D1258973

A
Joyful Meeting

Sexuality in Marriage

by Drs. Mike & Joyce Grace

International Marriage Encounter

A Joyful Meeting

ISBN 0-936098-29-5

© 1980 by International Marriage Encounter, Inc. All rights reserved. Printed in the United States of America. This book, or any portions thereof, may not be reproduced by any means without permission from the publisher: International Marriage Encounter, 955 Lake Drive, St. Paul, MN. 55120. Revised, 1981. Third Printing 1982. Fourth Printing 1984.

To Father Paul Gorieu, O.M.I.
He laid down his life for his friends—
but not before he put us all to work!

TABLE OF CONTENTS

FOREWORD

One morning in August, 1978, nearly a thousand married couples gathered in a huge auditorium in Milwaukee, Wisconsin. It was the occasion of a conference organized by the National Marriage Encounter. The entire morning was to be devoted to the subject of marital sex, presented by a Canadian husband/wife couple, both of whom were physicians.

Having ourselves participated in a great many conferences on sex, and listened to a multitude of speakers on the subject, we thought we knew what to expect—especially from physicians. There would be the usual biological explanations, the usual anatomical and physiological descriptions, the usual emphasis on pathology and dysfunction. It was all very familiar. We knew what was coming. All that was open to question was—"How will this particular audience take it?"

Our speakers, Drs. Mike and Joyce Grace, were introduced. Joyce responded with a warm, pleasant and quite unprofessional smile. Mike didn't smile. He startled us all by confessing that, confronted by this huge audience, he was feeling "scared to death." This was even more unprofessional.

During the next three hours, with one break, the audience listened. Joyce, perhaps to give Mike time to get over his nervousness, started in by talking about love between a man and woman, about how they express affection and caress each other. She described it all so sensitively and so understandingly that we soon felt as if she were talking directly to us. It was as unlike a professional lecture as anything we could imagine. It was conversational, and generously sprinkled with delightful touches of humor. What she said was at times quite profound, yet it came over with so much caring and compassion that we felt completely understood. Any sense of discomfort in the audience was soon entirely gone.

Then Mike took a turn. Now, we thought, we're going to get the heavy stuff. Not so. Mike adopted the same approach, with equal wisdom and insight, and even more sly humor.

By the time the morning was over, they had the huge audience in the hollow of their hands. We were all completely relaxed, comfortable, and grateful. Our sexuality seemed the most natural thing in the world, a beautiful gift from God that offered us love and joy. It seemed unbelievable that other people could have gotten it all so twisted up, so far out of its proper perspective.

Half a year later, we received the good news that the material presented at the Milwaukee conference was to be published, and we were invited to write a Foreword. We do so with the greatest pleasure, not only because we have such happy memories of Mike and Joyce on that August morning, but also because we have in the meantime been to Winnipeg, their home community, met them there, and found them to be just as genuine, sincere, and unpretentious in a personal encounter as they were up on the stage.

We can say without hesitation that the Graces presented the most gratifying program on marital sexuality that we have ever experienced. Their wisdom is profound, their insight unusually sensitive. They know how to blend sexuality and spirituality so that they naturally belong together. They look far beyond the stereotyped concepts as they communicate their understanding of the real meaning of fidelity, of the relationship between sex and love, of the real but subtle gender differences and how they may be blended in the complementarity of creative interaction.

Here, then, is marital sexuality explained in clear, simple, refreshing everyday language, and with a joyful rippling vein of humor which stands in vivid contrast to the dull, pompous, technical jargon that is all too often the only style the sex "experts" know how to use.

What more can we say? What more do we need to say? Read it for yourself, and you'll see what we mean!

David and Vera Mace
Founders of ACME,
Association of Couples
for Marriage Enrichment

PREFACE

This a small book about a big subject — sexuality. We don't attempt to deal with sexuality in general. Rather, our focus is on the part sexuality plays in the husband-wife relationship — and in particular on its potential for giving rise to conflict in this relationship.

This in no way implies a spirit of gloom and doom. We see these very conflicts as gifts from the Father, designed to help us grow in love and faith, designed to help prepare us for union with Him. In His plan, there is no Good Friday without an Easter; in the end it is joy and laughter that claim the victory.

CHAPTER 1

YOU MEAN WE'RE NOT THE SAME?

When we married more than 28 years ago, there were two things of which we were sure. One was that there were no significant differences between men and women beyond the obvious physical ones. The other was that our sexual relationship would be pure delight — no problems! And for eighteen carefree months thereafter we had no reason to question these certainties. There was, of course, some lack of technical finesse in our lovemaking, but we knew that this would come with practice — and this we were more than willing to do!

But then our lives entered what Eric Erikson has called

"the generative phase." We began our family and, coinciding with this, Mike took on the demanding task of establishing himself in general practice. Before long, beneath the surface courtesy and amiability, something was deeply, seriously wrong. Expectations and reality no longer coincided. Our sexual relationship, while it continued to provide physical pleasure, had become for both of us a source of deep emotional pain.

What had gone wrong? In our search for answers, we received no help from the professional "technocrats" — those doctors and behavioral scientists whose study of life is limited to text books and laboratories. But there is another rare breed of professional, the kind who learns about life from life. We encountered the occasional doctor or clergyman who had really listened to married people, taking seriously what they had to say. From these good listeners came a recurring opinion: "Men and woman are different."

It was an opinion we had previously brushed aside, but now we had run up against a hard, painful core of difference between the two of us. Not the general differences alleged in the old marriage manuals (things like "men are logical, women intuitive") but specific differences in things directly related to reproduction — home, children and, above all, sexual intercourse.

We had the good fortune to be in a position to compare our experience with that of many other couples. To our relief — and theirs — we found we were not alone. Now, after many years of trying to make sense of the experience of marriage (our own and that of many other couples) we have come to this conclusion: One of the things that gives the marriage relationship its special character compared to other friendships and other loves is that, in marriage, we must try to combine a psychological "love-friendship" relationship with an older (in the evolutionary sense) biological "mate" relationship. And we believe that one of the reasons why marriage is a school of love is that we often need to do some growing in the love-friendship department before we can handle the challenges that come out of our biological relationship.

2

MARRIAGE

PSYCHOLOGICAL	BIOLOGICAL
Love Friendship	"Mate" Relationship —pair-bonding —specialized (different) sexual behavior
Personal	Impersonal (System)

FIGURE 1

Of course we're not suggesting that the biological component of marriage contributes nothing but problems. On the contrary, it is the source of many delightful and creative things; in many ways it supports and strengthens our love. Pair-bonding reinforces fidelity. Our specialized (and therefore different) sexual characteristics are potentially complementary and enriching. And being mates and parents together gives married love a down-to-earth quality that is healthy. The challenges we face here test our love realistically; they don't allow us to live in a world of sentimental daydreams and illusions.

But some elements in our biology are potentially destructive of love. What comes naturally on the biological level is not always in the best interests of the persons involved — or of their relationship. There are times when biology pulls one way, while love would require us to go another. The source of the difficulty is our reproductive **specialization** as males and females — the fact that men and women come equipped, not only with different physical equipment for reproduction, but also with tendencies to feel and react differently in matters related to reproduction. Or, to put it another way, we say that they come equipped with differing reproductive drives.

3

CHAPTER 2

"THE REPRODUCTIVE DRIVE"

When we use the term "reproductive drive" we imply a **biological** influence on reproductive behavior. These are fighting words in some quarters. It is for some people an article of faith that human reproductive behavior is one hundred percent the product of cultural conditioning. While this is theoretically possible, it seems to us improbable. Specific reproductive behavior is part of the biological survival kit of all other species. It seems unlikely that the human species alone would lack this equipment.

At the same time we recognize the tremendous power of cultural conditioning and learning. Certainly this conditioning has, in the past, greatly exaggerated any biological differences between the sexes and even created differences that probably have no biological basis. We are aware that it would be equally possible to use cultural conditioning in the opposite way — to counteract the influence of biology, making men and women more alike. We recognize also that technology (notably contraception and safe alternatives to breast feeding) makes it possible to alter key elements in our reproductive programming. Such radical change in one part of the system could well cause changes in other parts. It follows that even differences that have a biological basis between the sexes are not immune to change.

With these reservations in mind, let's look at Figure 2 and consider what we suggest is the probable pattern of the inborn, biological reproductive drive in the human species (and to a large extent among mammals generally, though nature is always full of variety and exceptions). Note that we refer to this as the **probable** pattern of the reproductive drive. We're not suggesting this as infallible scientific dogma. Rather, it's what a scientist would call our "working hypothesis." It helps to account for the facts as we now know them, and it's **useful,** useful in making sense of sexuality at the practical level.

Referring then to Figure 2, we see first that males and females are programmed to spend their sexual energy differently. Note that "sexual energy" does not refer to the person's **total** energy, but only to that part of it which is geared to procreation and the nurturing of offspring. The male's sexual energy is spent mostly **outside** the nest, competing with other males for status and dominance, fulfilling his role as provider and protector. The female's sexual energy, on the other hand, is spent mostly **within** the nest, providing the necessary environment for her offspring, bearing, nurturing and training them.

REPRODUCTIVE DRIVE

	MALE	**FEMALE**
Total sexual energy	Mostly focused OUTSIDE the "nest"	Mostly focused WITHIN the "nest"
Sexual energy within nest-mate-offspring area	Mostly focused on COITUS	Mostly focused on — nesting — maternal activities Focus on coitus is CONDITIONAL
Reproductive bond	Primarily to MATE, established, reinforced by coitus	Primarily to nest, offspring
Focus in relation to mate	Strong focus on COITUS	Main focus on —protection —security Focus on coitus CONDITIONAL

FIGURE 2

Looking next at the second line of Figure 2, we see that when the male does appear on the home front, the main focus of his sexual energy is on coitus* with his mate. The female's main focus, however, is on her nesting and maternal activities. There's a focus on coitus as well, but it's conditional on her mate fulfilling his role as protector, provider and co-parent. Applying this in a human context — unless a man is a good friend to his wife and a responsible father, we're likely to find her playing with the kids until they go to bed, then locking herself up in the bathroom for a three-hour bubble-bath until she's sure her husband is asleep. Coitus in that household is like the Dodo bird, something you can read about in books, but not something that still exists.

*Coitus — the biological act of mating or copulation — the insertion of the penis into the vagina with the release of semen there.

In the third line of Figure 2, we compare the reproductive bond in male and female. We see that in the male this bond is primarily to his mate. Coitus helps to establish this bond initially, and continues to reinforce it. Incidentally, most biologists would agree that the biological purpose of most coitus that takes place in the human species is not procreation, which is rarely possible, but reinforcing of the pair-bond to favor lasting, monogamous mating. In contrast, the reproductive bond in the female is primarily to her nest and to her offspring.

Finally, in the last line of Figure 2, we see that the focus of the male in relation to his mate is on coitus — on his mate as a sexual partner. In the female, however, her primary focus is on her mate as a provider, protector, and partner in caring for the young. She has a focus on coitus too — but only under certain conditions.

We hasten to qualify what we've been saying. When we talk about this reproductive drive, we are talking about only one influence on personality. There are hundreds of ingredients that go into making each one of us a unique individual. The reproductive drive is concerned with only one dimension of life — reproduction. Even there it's not the whole story. We have mentioned already that human beings, unlike animals, are greatly influenced by education and culture; these other influences may either exaggerate, modify, or cancel-out biological tendencies. So we can't say, "Men are like this; women are like that." We can only say that men will have a **tendency** to be like this, women a **tendency** to be like that, because of the biological influences giving them a push in different directions.

We should also point out that the strength of this reproductive drive varies due to many factors. One important variable is the stage of the marriage relationship. This reproductive drive pattern is not noticeable at the honeymoon stage. It may not be obvious during the retirement years. As one would expect, it makes itself felt most strongly during the active child-bearing and child-rearing years.

Finally, we want to stress that, in describing these reproductive drive patterns, we are not presenting them as models or ideals of masculine and feminine behavior. These patterns are designed to ensure the **physical survival** of our species. But, as human beings, we are called to, are hungry for, and capable of, much more than just physical survival. Our reproductive instincts can't be depended upon to provide for these other dimensions. That's up to the part of us that can think and make choices. The main reason we think it's important to be aware of our biological programming is that such awareness is the first step in bringing this part of our being under the discipline of love.

There are other advantages to being aware of these biological influences. When we understand the "why" of our sexual differences, we can accept them more peacefully. If we recognize that we were born programmed to be this way (just as we were born programmed to have big feet, short noses, or curly hair), we are more inclined to adjust to our differences matter-of-factly, as we do to the weather and to other things over which we have no control. We are less likely to feel angry with ourselves and with each other when our differences cause inconvenience.

Another advantage in knowing the source of our differences is that we will be less tempted to pass unfair judgment on ourselves, or on each other. Men have often been judged animalistic and selfish because of the nature of their reproductive drive with its rather urgent focus on coitus. On the other hand, the female drive, with its strong focus on nest and children, and less than compelling focus on coitus, has been interpreted as evidence that women are by nature more loving and more "spiritual." Or sometimes women have been labelled "frigid" or "not real women" because their attitudes toward sexual intercourse were not mirror images of their husbands'. Yet these differences are simply biological characteristics; they tell us nothing about a person's capacity for love or sensitivity to things of the spirit. Knowing this, we are much less likely to make them the basis for harsh judgments.

Finally, understanding these basic differences in reproductive drive helps us to understand, and therefore to deal with, certain practical differences we are likely to experience in marriage. Let's look at three of these practical differences.

9

CHAPTER 3

THE DIFFERENT FACES OF INFIDELITY

When we talk here about infidelity we're not referring to adultery, which is a relatively uncommon and secondary form of infidelity. Our marriage vow isn't just a vow to avoid adultery. It is a vow to live as one in love. We become unfaithful any time we quit trying to live this vow — any time we settle for a life of chronic selfishness, of doing our own thing at the expense of our love and unity as a couple. This kind of infidelity often wears a mask of respectability and responsibility. The form it takes often reflects the influence of the reproductive drive. For this reason, infidelity tends to wear different disguises in husbands as compared to wives.

The selfish male is usually found devoting himself one hundred percent to being a big operator in the outside world. This could be in the world of work, of politics, or perhaps some kind of apostolic or community service, or it might be in sports, getting the old golf score down or his jogging distance up. If success in these areas eludes him, he may take refuge in the pub, swapping tall tales with other marital dropouts. (Or, if all else fails, we may find him out in the marsh, trying to outwit some poor dumb duck.) Whatever form his "big operator" complex takes outside the home, his performance on the home front is the same. He comes home to eat, to sleep, to change his socks (at least we hope so!) — and to have his sexual needs attended to. He considers his responsibilities ended when he's paid the bills.

The selfish female, on the other hand, is not likely to be

found paddling in the marsh or communing with cronies in the pub. She is more likely to be found concentrating her efforts on the care of the home and the children. This can apply even when she works outside the home. Women work for many reasons, but the most common one is financial, related to the standard of living they want to achieve in the home and for their children. She considers her responsibilities ended if she's a good housekeeper and a "good mother." We've used quotation marks, because she can't be a good mother unless she's a good wife; but she's not aware of this. She expects her husband to pay the bills, do the chores, help with the children in a way indicated by her — and otherwise stay out of her hair. She considers any personal demands on her by her husband too much — especially sexual demands — unless she herself is in the mood.

In both cases, these two tell themselves that they are acting out of love. He is knocking himself out to provide for the family or to build a nice community for the children to grow up in. She is knocking herself out so that they will have a lovely home and the children will have socks that match and not have dirty feet when the school nurse examines them. But if we compare the pattern of their lives with the patterns in Figure 2 (page 7) we see that they are simply doing what they are programmed to do by their reproductive drives.

The result is the family's **physical** needs are met all right; but everyone — husband, wife, childen — is being shortchanged **psychologically.** We are not suggesting that working to provide for the family's physical well-being is unimportant. Love will include this — and we are lucky that we have instincts to give us a push in this direction. But love will seek the **highest** good and, therefore, the psychological as well as the physical well-being of all the persons in the family. Love will require us to be aware, to think, to work at the art of loving, rather than merely to surrender our lives to blind instinct. We need continually to examine ourselves and our lifestyle to see if we are drifting into these very common patterns of infidelity — this doing what comes naturally at the instinctive level, to the neglect of the love-friendship relationship, which should be our main concern.

12

CHAPTER 4

THE RELATIONSHIP BETWEEN SEX AND LOVE

The second way in which our basic biological differences often result in some important practical differences is that there tends to be a different relationship between sex and love in the two sexes. This is probably the most important area of difference between men and women because of its great potential for messing up a marriage. Yet ignorance of this difference is the rule rather than the exception. Love and sex are either equated or else considered to be totally unrelated. The result is tremendous misunderstanding, confusion, pain and bitterness. Yet when we understand the true relationship between sex and love in both sexes, we have a powerful tool for building love and confidence in one another. So we encourage you to pay close attention to this chapter.

PRIMARY INSTINCTIVE LOVE SOURCE

	MALE	**FEMALE**
Instinctive Love SOURCE	Love/Sex	Love/Protection Love/Security Love/Cooperation
Instinctive Love NEED	Sexual Acceptance	Protection Security Valued

FIGURE 3

Looking then at Figure 3, let's consider first the Primary Instinctive Love Source. In the male, this is a "Love/Sex" source; he relates to his mate primarily as a sexual partner. So the biological foundation for a man's love for his wife is sexual attraction. This is the initial stimulus for, and one of the cornerstones of, the ensuing love relationship. This is how the male initially "locks on" to this particular woman. When you add to this the specifically human dimension of

13

love, you then have a blending of love and sex. So we say that the Primary Instinctive Love Source of a man is a "Love/Sex" source. The biological roots of his love are in sexual desire. It was there first, and will always be a powerful part of his love for his wife.

In a woman, the specifically human dimension of love is built upon a different biological foundation. Her Primary Instinctive Love Source is found in sensing the man's general air of being "sympatico" — his sensitivity, his cooperation, the security and protection that he offers her and his support of their mutual goals. Sexual desire here is conditional and variable. Her feelings for her husband can be friendly and affectionate, without there necessarily being any element of sexual desire.

So there is a possibility of confusion. The wife thinks, "Why can't there be physical affection without it always ending up with sex?" She interprets her husband's poor track record in this Platonic love routine as a sign that he really doesn't love her. At the same time her husband interprets his wife's lack of sexual interest as a lack of love and concern. It's hard for a man to imagine feeling and being affectionate without at the same time feeling some degree of desire. So if the couple continues to function only at this instinctive level (and it's amazing how many people do), they will repeatedly hurt each other and cause doubts and fears in this most basic part of their lives.

Let's consider now the Primary Instinctive Love Need in both sexes (bottom line, Figure 3). In the male, the Primary Instinctive Love Need, and almost a prerequisite for love, is **sexual acceptance.** In the female, the Primary Instinctive Love Need, and again almost the prerequisite for love, is an atmosphere of security and protection, of companionship and friendship, and the certain knowledge of being valued and cherished.

Throughout our lives each sex obviously needs lots of both. The **wife** needs sexual acceptance; the **husband** needs the atmosphere of security, companionship and friendship. And if both the husband and wife are getting lots of both love-needs, the difference in primary love-need isn't impor-

14

tant. So when things are going well in the marriage generally, the difference is not a source of conflict. But when other
problems arise, these differences suddenly become important; they begin to hurt the relationship.

Sexual acceptance is the starting point for the male; it
conditions and determines his response to the female. Let's
look at an example of this. In the animal kingdom, there are
bands of wild horses. In these bands, the stallion must be accepted as a stallion before he provides any protection and
security for the mares. So if there is a bad-tempered mare
that bites at him and kicks at him any time he wanders by in
the spring or summer looking for a piece of grass he is going to get the message, which is: "Get lost you big slob!"
Then when the snow is deep and the wolves start to howl,
she is going to be on her own, and they will find only her
bones the following spring. This is the inevitable result of
her behavior because, since there is no sexual acceptance on
her part, there is no bonding on the stallion's part and,
therefore, no protection.

Similarly, a mare must feel secure with the stallion before
she becomes a part of his band. If he is a scrawny little guy
with a slew-foot or if he is clumsy and always falling into
gopher holes or getting his head caught in the branches of
the trees while going through the brush, he is obviously a
loser and, automatically, a celibate. And if he is also stupid
on top of all this — if he spends half of his life with his nose
full of porcupine quills because he keeps forgetting what
that little brown thing did the last time he tried to push it
out of a tree, he is going to be a celibate for sure. The
mares really can't feel secure with a stumble-bum like this.
(We always hasten to add that we are not inferring that all
celibates are stumble-bums. We know many of them can tell
a pine cone from a porcupine!) In humans, lack of protection
may take a different form. The husband is physically able to
protect his wife (he doesn't fall into gopher holes and he
keeps his nose clean); but, he is not willing to protect her
psychologically. This obvious lack of care and concern
strikes a very heavy blow against her love source. She can't
feel secure with someone who obviously doesn't care that
much.

15

Thus we see that the Primary Instinctive Love Needs of the male and female are different. The man's primary need is to be accepted sexually. If he doesn't feel loved here he doesn't feel loved at all. He will feel used and abused and will bitterly resent all the so called Platonic demands that his wife makes on him. The woman's primary need is to feel loved and accepted in the total situation of life in which she finds herself. If she doesn't feel loved here she doesn't feel loved at all. She will feel used and abused and will bitterly resent sex and all its demands. These reactions of hostility are inevitable. When one feels rejected and used and abused, it is virtually impossible to reach out repeatedly in love to the other whom you think is using and abusing and rejecting you.

When we are dealing with married couples with problems, we usually ask them four simple questions:
1) Are you happily married?
2) Does your spouse love you?
3) What do you think about him/her?
4) How do you feel about him/her?

Almost invariably the husband's answers will depend on his experience in the area of sexual acceptance, while the wife's answers will depend on her experiences in the areas of being secure, precious, protected and appreciated.

Sometimes the dialogue is the stuff of which text books are made:

"Do you think your wife really loves you?"
"Hell no! She hasn't let me put a hand on her in three months!"
"Do you think your husband really loves you?"
"Oh, my no! — All he ever thinks about is sex!!! I know he loves the dog because he treats him so well and so differently from me."

This is tragic, because what should draw them closer together, **by its very nature** is helping to destroy their relationship. You can see the ease with which a vicious circle can develop and this is certainly the beginning of the end for a lot of marriages. We call this a "negative cycle." It is illustrated in Figure 4.

16

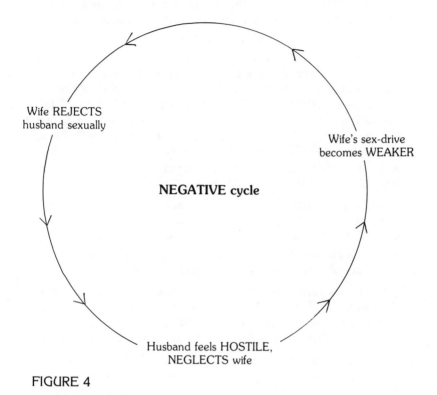

Wife REJECTS
husband sexually

Wife's sex-drive
becomes WEAKER

NEGATIVE cycle

Husband feels HOSTILE,
NEGLECTS wife

FIGURE 4

Sometimes it starts with the husband feeling that he is being short-changed sexually. Actually he may be doing quite
well; but he is being greedy. He interprets the lack of enthusiasm on his wife's part as rejection. Of course, this makes
him hostile. He then neglects his wife more in all the little
ways that mean so much to her. This neglect threatens her
love source, the knowledge that she is secure, that she is
valued, precious and special. When her love source has been
threatened for any length of time, she begins to doubt, to
feel unloved. When she feels that her husband does not love
her, her sex drive becomes weaker, her response is poor,
and she rejects him sexually. The husband, now running true
to form, interprets this rejection as a sign that she does not

17

love him. This is even further proof that he has been taken, that he is being used. He becomes more hostile and neglects his wife more and more. The cycle is underway.

Sometimes it is the wife who comes to the realization that she is being **emotionally** short-changed; that she is being used, that she is being treated as a "thing" — part of his equipment in the house. She realizes that he has his hi-fi in the basement, his color TV in the living room and her in the bedroom. When this realization occurs to her, her instinctive love source is threatened. She must then say to herself, "I am not special; I am just another popular brand — Panasonic, Zenith and me, Mabel!"

When this realization strikes her, all sorts of things start to hit the fan — because this shatters her instinctive love source. She is not secure, valued, protected and precious; so she does not feel loved. She is hurt and angry and, in anger, will certainly reject her husband sexually.

In his ignorance, he interprets this rejection as a sign that she does not love him. He reacts in his usual stupid way and neglects her even more, and her love source is threatened even more. The terrible negative cycle gets underway again.

This mess is the inevitable result of the failure to realize the different relationships between love and sex in the two sexes. Because of these different relationships, we find the interpretations differ tremendously. This is where the trouble starts because, when the wife rejects her husband, he regards the rejection as a sign of "no love." He reacts with neglect, which is interpreted as "no love" by his wife. She rejects him even more — and away we go.

This is the point to which many marriages have deteriorated before the couple comes in for any help. It is usually the wife who comes in first. If the couple still has the basic characteristics of love, if they can learn to communicate with each other, to tell each other their wants, needs and hurts, then the marriage can be salvaged. The husband should be able to say: "I feel hurt when you dodge me. I feel crushed when you insult me, or reject me. I feel sick inside when you don't respond at all, or when you say, 'For God's sake, hurry up and get finished, I have to get

18

some sleep.' " If she accepts these as valid complaints, then the couple is at least up to square one.

Similarly, the wife may say "When you ignore me the whole evening and then come to bed and grab me without any tenderness or love, you make me feel like a prostitute. I am hurt, and embarrassed and angry and sometimes I think I would like to kill you." If her husband is a sensitive and perceptive chap, he will realize she is really trying to tell him something. He should then realize that there is much work to be done in this marriage.

Then they can begin to construct a positive cycle in their relationship. He will ensure that, on his part, there is increased **emotional** input. When this happens, his wife's instinctive needs will be met. She will feel secure and special. She will sense this cooperation and willingness to help and to

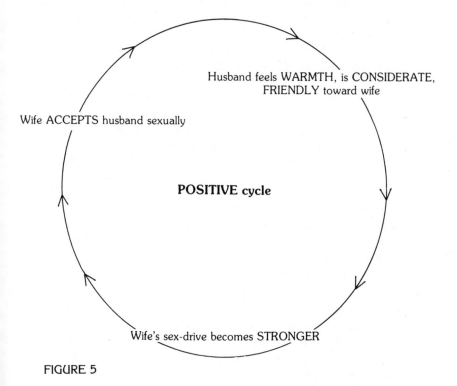

FIGURE 5

19

please. She will say, "This is how it is supposed to be. This clown really does love me. My mother **was** wrong!"

Then she is much more ready to accept him sexually. She will become more interested in sex and the sex drive will become stronger as she realizes its immediate rewards. This change may come as quite a surprise to her husband and he will say to himself: "Gee! I struck oil here somewhere. I am finally doing something right!" He responds to this warmth from his wife, and is more friendly toward her. His increased emotional input, of course, will reinforce her knowledge that this guy really does love her. And so it is only onward and upward from there.

Sometimes it is the wife who, after an honest self-appraisal of her track record, will have to admit that she has been dragging her feet. She has to accept the fact that sex is not just a spectator sport — it's not like watching "Monday Night Football" or "Wide World of Sports." She must also accept the fact that, when she just lies there, doing it from memory, as it were, or looking out the window with a mouth full of sunflower seeds, she is really communicating a lot to her husband. She is saying, "I don't give a damn about you." So for the sake of her marriage and because she really loves her husband, she makes the extra effort and accepts him sexually. This acceptance means love with a capital "L" for her husband; so he becomes warmer and more considerate and friendly. This change confirms his love for his wife and things start to move. Her sex drive becomes stronger because she feels and reacts to his warmth and friendship. She realizes that sex is "really not that bad." Her interest in sex increases. She accepts him sexually more readily and much more frequently. Then the husband says, "Gee, I've struck the mother lode here. Things are great. Now if I can only learn to pace myself, we can go on forever!"

Again we stress that **both** men and women need to feel accepted sexually — **both** need to feel precious and special and secure. The difference is one of priorities and emphasis. And it is specifically in this marriage situation that they can complement each other's strengths and meet each other's needs — and so help themselves to "live happily ever after."

CHAPTER 5

PATTERNS OF RESPONSE DURING SEXUAL INTERCOURSE

There is another area in which our basic biological differences are likely to result in some very practical differences. That is in the way we function with respect to sexual intercourse itself.

But before getting into this, we need to clarify some terms. Many people, when referring to sexual intercourse, just mean coitus. But that is not what we mean when we use this term. If we use the term coitus we are referring to the time when the penis is actually in the vagina. When we talk about **sexual intercourse,** we have in mind the whole lovemaking process — the psychological arousal, the foreplay, coitus, the afterplay (which may be necessary to bring the wife to orgasm if she hasn't reached it during coitus) and the time of afterglow. Another term we use is **erotic.** We use it to describe the special feelings that are connected with sexual intercourse, the kind that climax in orgasm. Erotic feelings are sexual, but not all sexual feelings are erotic. So sometimes it is handy to have this little word, erotic, to indicate the specific kind of sexual feeling we are talking about. And from the word, erotic, comes the adjective **erogenous** which we use when talking about the erogenous zones, or those parts of the body that give rise to erotic feelings.

We can go on now to describe the different ways in which men and women are likely to function with respect to sexual intercourse. We do this in considerable detail because, although married couples have usually experienced these patterns, they are often not at all sure that what they have experienced is normal. We hope that by the end of this chapter such couples will be saying: "Isn't it great to know that we're normal!"

We will begin with the patterns of response in the **young** man and the **young** woman — starting with that in the young male.

Pattern in the Young Male

The young male's pattern is usually rather simple, standardized and uncomplicated. He is likely to be self-starting and quite easily aroused. **Psychological stimulation** alone (for example, just looking forward to coitus) is often sufficient to arouse him fully to the point where he needs no further preparation for coitus. In his case, foreplay is almost certain to have an erotic effect because he is easily aroused.

Coitus in a man is **guaranteed** to be an intensely erotic experience because it is physically impossible otherwise. If there's no erotic feeling, there's no erection; and if there's no erection, there's no coitus. So, in the case of the male, there is a built-in connection between coitus and erotic feeling. There is also a strong built-in connection between coitus and orgasm. Coitus can simply continue until orgasm occurs or desire is lost.

Orgasm in both sexes is an **involuntary** process. It is not something that we can directly produce — or prevent — by deciding that we would like to. But this lack of control over orgasm becomes noticeable in different ways in men as compared to women. In a young man the problem is likely to be the inability to **prevent** or **postpone** orgasm, resulting in premature ejaculation which is really premature orgasm. Premature ejaculation is so common that it is probably a misnomer to call it premature (implying that it is somehow abnormal). In the rest of the animal kingdom, instant ejaculation is the rule. It is only in our species that males learn to engage in coitus for an extended length of time, postponing orgasm. It's something that can be learned, but it isn't something that seems to come naturally — or easily — to most young men. Sometimes orgasm will occur

22

as soon as, or even before, coitus begins. More often it comes during coitus but sooner than the man would have planned if he had had a little more control over the situation. Unfortunately, the harder the man tries to prevent his orgasm, the faster it is likely to come. Feelings of tension and anxiety tend to bring things on sooner rather than later.

Once orgasm occurs, the most common pattern is that the male's erection subsides and further coitus becomes physically impossible for a time. He will need a rest period of variable length — anywhere from minutes to days, depending on how lively he is — before he is ready for full-scale action again. He needs this time to recharge his batteries before he can have another erection and engage in coitus again.

Patterns in the Young Female

When we turn our attention to the pattern of response in the young woman we find a much more complex and variable situation.

Why this difference? There are several biological reasons, some of which we have already considered. In Chapter 2, we noted that the drive toward coitus has a relatively low priority in the reproductive instincts of the female as compared to the male. As a result, it's often as if women were operating on a weaker power source, a smaller battery, when it comes to sexual intercourse, because less of their reproductive energy is being channelled in this direction. This applies especially when much of a woman's sexual energy is being absorbed by maternal functions. Then in Chapter 4, we noted the importance of the overall emotional climate. If this climate is bad, not only is there likely to be an absence of desire — there is frequently a strong aversion to sexual intimacy. In addition to these factors with which we are already familiar, there are two other biological sources of difference.

There are, first of all, important consequences that flow simply from the differences in sexual mechanics. We have seen that, for mechanical reasons, coitus without desire is physically impossible for a man. But this is not the case with women. For a woman, coitus is something that can happen to her in any condition. She can be unconscious. She can be planning her spring wardrobe. She can be wondering if the stew is burning. Her mind and her feelings can be on the far side of the moon — but it is still physically possible for coitus to take place. Life being as odd as it is, over the course of 50 years of marriage, coitus is likely to happen to a woman in almost an infinite variety of emotional states. Her physical response will vary accordingly. So, in women, the connection between coitus and erotic feeling is not something that can be taken for granted; it has to be arranged. Another result of the mechanical difference is that it is more likely that coitus will be an **incomplete** erotic experience for a woman. She may become aroused and be moving in the direction of orgasm, but coitus ends before her orgasm occurs. There are two reasons for this. The obvious one is that the duration of coitus depends on when the husband has his orgasm; it is not affected by whether or not his wife has had one. The other reason is that the kind of stimulation a woman receives during coitus is often less effective in bringing her to orgasm than the kind of stimulation a man receives. The most effective way to bring a male to orgasm is to stimulate the penis. And, of course, the penis is **directly** stimulated during coitus. The most effective way to bring a woman to orgasm is to stimulate the clitoris. But the clitoris is only **indirectly** stimulated during coitus itself — and, in some positions, may receive very little stimulation. So the simple difference in mechanics is a tremendous source of difference in sexual experience and response in the two sexes.

The final important biological source of difference is that men and women have different sexual histories. They have different ways of learning their feelings about and responses to sexual intercourse. Most men in their early teens will begin to experience erections and nocturnal emissions (wet dreams) which are like previews or rehearsals for sexual intercourse. These are positive experiences. They feel good and make a man feel good about himself. So he learns very early, from what happens automatically in his own body, to have positive feelings and a strong desire for sexual intercourse.

24

In a woman, the changes that take place in her body when she becomes sexually mature do not teach her anything about sexual intercourse. **She will learn her responses and feelings only as she becomes sexually active,** whether through masturbation or sexual activity with someone else. This means, first of all, that she may begin to learn her responses much later than the average male. If she has refrained from any kind of sexual activity before marriage, she will only be beginning to learn her feelings about sexual intercourse on the honeymoon. Until then, it has simply been outside her experience. She probably knows about it in her head, but for her body and for her feelings it has had no reality, no meaning. It also means that the way she learns to feel about sexual intercourse can vary a lot, depending on what her past experience has been. If it has been pleasurable she will have learned to feel a desire for more. If her past experience has been painful, or even if it has been indifferent — not painful, but not rewarding either — she will have come to look upon sexual intercourse as something she prefers to avoid. It may take months — even years — of good sexual experiences before a woman develops a full positive response to sexual intercourse, and especially to coitus. A response to foreplay seems to come more ready made; but a full vaginal response to coitus requires more learning. Many women who have been married for years have never learned to enjoy sexual intercourse for the same reason that they have never learned to play the violin — they have never had the proper opportunity to learn, the right learning situation. Given the right learning situation and conditions, they can still learn, although the learning process will probably be complicated by the need to heal indifferent or unhappy sexual memories from the past.

All these sources of difference can add up to quite a different pattern of response in a young woman as compared to a young man. The young woman is likely to be slower to become aroused, less likely to be self-starting. In her case, psychological stimulation is very important as the **first stage** in the arousal process; but, generally, this will only **begin** the process. She is likely to need intensive and prolonged physical stimulation of the kind we call foreplay

25

before she is fully aroused and ready for coitus. And there is no guarantee that this foreplay will arouse desire. If there is competition from other things — distractions, other feelings — foreplay may have no erotic effect. This is why we emphasize that the **most important erogenous zone is the brain.** Unless it is turned on to erotic feeling, the other erogenous zones won't work in an erotic way. So there is no guarantee that going through the mechanics of foreplay will arouse a woman whose master switch is less easily turned on than that of the average male.

This can be very puzzling to husbands. They go out and buy themselves one of those "Do-It-Yourself: How-To-Be-A-Great-Lover" books. They follow the instructions to the letter — and nothing happens. They look at the lady, look at the book — and wonder which one they should try to take back! The situation can be compared to a house in which the main power switch is off. You can run around plugging in kettles and flipping switches until you are loop-legged — but nothing will happen until that main power source comes on. It's not just a simple on or off switch; it's more like a rheostat. The power comes on only gradually and, until the power is fully on, the intensely erogenous zones will not function in an erotic way. If you try to use them, you just blow a fuse. Unfortunately, getting that master-switch turned on is complicated by the fact that women tend to be easily distracted throughout the whole love-making process. Some cynic has remarked: "If there is anything else to think about, she probably will!"

We have already mentioned that a woman's full response to coitus is often acquired only with favorable sexual experience over a period of months or even years. Even after a full response to coitus has developed, on each occasion she is likely to be slower than her husband to focus on and to desire coitus, as well as slower to become fully prepared for coitus. She will still need **intensive** foreplay before she is fully aroused, before she is physically prepared. It requires intense erotic feeling to produce the special lubrication and the other physical changes that are necessary before she will have a full response to coitus.

26

Then even if she has been well prepared by foreplay before coitus, she is likely to be slower to reach her climax during coitus — so much so that, unless she has been brought to the brink of orgasm before coitus begins, orgasm is unlikely to occur during coitus unless her husband is unusually durable and skillful.

As in the male, orgasm in women is involuntary; but her problem is not likely to be difficulty in **postponing** orgasm, but difficulty in **reaching** it. Again, anxiously striving just makes things worse. As soon as she starts to **work** at producing an orgasm, erotic feeling goes out the window and she is back to square one.

The male's difficulty in postponing orgasm and the female's difficulty in reaching it is obviously a bad combination. It is some consolation to know that it's par for the course, especially in the early months and years of marriage (though by no means limited to that period). The latest figures that we have heard for the duration of coitus that favors a woman reaching orgasm is 15 minutes or longer — whereas the national average for duration of coitus is two-and-a-half-minutes. So if you are having problems in this area, we hope you don't think you are alone.

Anyway, the important thing is to relax and not worry about it. It is something that will tend to work itself out in time. Age and experience will help the husband slow down, the wife speed up. Presumably if they live long enough, somewhere they will meet.

Meanwhile, it's not a disaster. If coitus ends before the wife has her orgasm, her husband can stimulate the clitoris afterwards — **or whatever else his wife desires in the way of stimulation** — to bring her to orgasm. And, of course, the wife herself can do this, if the husband is not gentleman enough to do so. But we certainly hope that her husband will be gallant enough to finish what he has started.

One practical tip: the husband will have a longer fuse if it hasn't been too long since his previous orgasm. So if a couple has intercourse twice within a relatively short period, there may be hope for a little more durability the second time.

27

Orgasm is the most common climax of erotic feeling in women. Sometimes, though, women will instead reach a high level of erotic feeling, stay there for a time, and then the erotic feeling subsides without orgasm. And they say that they are perfectly happy about the whole thing. If they say they are happy about it, everyone else should be happy too.

It is our impression that the intensity of orgasm varies from woman to woman in a way that it apparently doesn't from man to man. We say this because some women report that their orgasms are earth shaking; others complain that theirs are rather ho-hum affairs. Someone has suggested the comparison with a sneeze. A sneeze, you will be fascinated to know, is an "orgasm of the nose." So, if you don't get anything else out of this chapter, you should enjoy sneezing more from now on. And just as there are some sneezes that rattle the windows and others that are kitten soft, there seem to be similar variations in the intensity of female orgasm. You don't get the same kind of feedback from men; so either they don't experience this variation or else they don't talk about it!

It is also our impression that orgasm is probably less important in at least some women's scheme of things than all the present fuss over it would suggest. It is, for them, one of many nice things connected with sexual intercourse, but not always or necessarily the most important. We say this because many women report that they can and do enjoy sexual intercourse without necessarily desiring or experiencing orgasm. We don't suggest that it's unimportant, but perhaps not so all-important as the present emphasis on it tends to suggest.

Following orgasm, the usual pattern is probably similar to that of the male. Since the famous Masters and Johnson study of female sexual response we've been hearing a lot about something they called "multiple orgasm." We have been puzzled by this, because it didn't seem to correspond to the clinical experience of doctors with considerable background in this field. Now, according to the latest information we have, it seems that it's been a case of "much ado about nothing." It is now being reported that what Masters and Johnson called multiple orgasms is what other people have been describing for years as **orgasmic peaks,** or **clitoral peaks.** An orgasmic peak is an incomplete orgasm; the orgasmic process begins but is reversed before going on to completion in the final resolution phase. A woman can experience a succession of these peaks without loss of erotic interest and feeling. However, once she experiences a complete orgasm that moves on to the final resolution phase, this is followed by a pattern similar to that we have described in the male — relaxation, time needed to "recharge her battery" before being capable of a full response again. As one woman described it, "I can experience several peaks with clitoral stimulation, but only one big one, which usually, but not always, comes with insertion."

A final important characteristic of the young woman's pattern is that she is likely to have a smaller sexual appetite than the male. Once the initial curiosity and novelty of the honeymoon is past, she is likely to desire — and be capable of — a full sexual response less often than her husband. This becomes more pronounced during the active childbearing and childrearing phase of the marriage.

When we add all this up, it becomes clear that sexual intercourse can mean many different kinds of experience for a woman. It depends on the emotional climate — whether it is one of affection, hostility or boredom. It depends on the setting. And here, the presence or absence of distractions is terribly important. It depends on her sexual appetite or lack of it at the time. It depends on her age and past sexual experience. It also depends on her husband's skill as a lover, in the areas of both psychological and physical seduction.

Her physical response to coitus can vary enormously. If she has been fully aroused by foreplay before coitus — almost to the point of orgasm — and if coitus lasts long enough, she is likely to have a full response to coitus, probably climaxing in orgasm. If she has been only partially aroused before coitus, she is likely to have a mild erotic response. Full arousal and orgasm during coitus is much less likely, unless the clitoris is being stimulated at the same time. If she has been not at all aroused erotically before coitus, she is likely to have little or no erotic response to coitus. Coitus should not be physically unpleasant, however, if two conditions are met: first of all, if there is a warm emotional climate and, secondly, if coitus does not go on for too long. If it continues for too long, the lack of special lubrication starts to cause friction and discomfort — and even pain. (Fortunately artificial lubricants are a help in getting around this difficulty; ordinary baby oil works well.) Finally, if there is no desire plus a negative emotional climate, coitus can be physically unpleasant and even painful.

Because of the many factors influencing feminine response and because a wide variation in response is normal, it is time we dropped the judgmental labels "frigid" and "frigidity." We must begin to think in terms that take into account the **why** of a lack of physical response in an individual case. As we have seen, there are many possibilities.

Before leaving our discussion of the feminine pattern of response, we should probably say something about the Masters and Johnson study of human sexual response. This study has been much publicized — and, unfortunately, much misinterpreted (not by Masters and Johnson, but by others only vaguely familiar with their work). Their research did not attempt to examine sexuality in the broad sense that we are dealing with it here; it was concerned only with the **physiology** of sexual response, with the measurable physical changes that take place during sexual arousal and orgasm. For this they didn't need subjects whose overall pattern of sexuality was typical; they needed subjects willing and able to perform sexually on schedule and under research conditions. The subjects were, first of all, paid volunteers; this alone would exclude most average or typical people. To be considered for the study, volunteers had to report extensive sexual activity (both masturbation and sexual intercourse); they also had to report that they became aroused and reached orgasm easily and frequently. Of the women selected, half were subsequently dropped — leaving the half that were able to perform most efficiently under the rather bizarre conditions of the study. Clearly these were not "typical" women. Yet there has been a strong tendency to make their responses the standard by which other women are judged. The result is that many normal women have felt sexually inadequate. Even worse, they have had to suffer their husband's judgment that they were sub-standard specimens of womanhood.

We don't suggest that the women in this study were **abnormal** — only that they were not **average,** or **typical.** They came from one extreme, not the middle, of the wide range of what is sexually normal. This brings us to our next point.

In describing the patterns of response in the two sexes, we have been speaking in broad generalities. Not all of you will recognize yourselves in these patterns; in fact, some of you may find that, to some extent, you experience these patterns **in reverse.** This is to be expected — both because of non-biological influences and because, even biologically, there is wide individual variation. A good comparison here is with another biological characteristic — height. It is true to say that men, on the average, are taller than women; but there are some women who are as tall as — or taller than — some men. So while in most marriages the husband is taller than his wife, in some cases the wife is the taller, and in still others husband and wife are about the same size. There is nothing abnormal about these last two situations — they are simply less common or typical. The same thing applies to the less typical sexual combinations.

Another qualification is that we have been describing the patterns that are common in younger men and women. These patterns tend to change as we grow older.

Changes in the Later Years

Like all the body functions, the sexual function in a man slows down and becomes less vigorous, less pressing and less urgent as he grows older. This doesn't mean that it stops nor that it's about to stop — so there's no need to panic and try to get in as much mileage as possible before running out of gas. It's just slowing down. A healthy man of sixty can still jog. Even a feeble old man of 80 can still walk (especially with a tail wind or if he is going downhill). He may need a little help and encouragement, but he can still get over the road.

So it is with the sexual function of an older man. He may not go to the well as often, but he still enjoys the drink. The drink may be even sweeter, because he doesn't know when he will be back. He doesn't even know **if** he will be back.

A 72-year-old man from the Ozarks once explained this fact of life by saying: "I can't plow as much ground in a day as I could when I was 18, but I can still plow one furrow just as deep and as straight as ever I could."

In Figure 6, we have plotted the intensity of the sexual drive and pleasure against the time involved. We see the young man start off at zero, rise quickly to great heights and achieve his orgasm. The lights go out and the intensity of the drive then quickly falls to zero. The man of 60 also starts at zero, but you will notice he takes considerably more time and does not achieve the same intensity of drive and pleasure as the 20-year-old man. He also reaches a sort of a plateau prior to orgasm, after which the intensity of the drive falls off very quickly to zero. A 20-year-old looking at the graph of a 60-year-old will probably not be too impressed with the amount of enjoyment involved, but every 60-year-old man will realize that, although his experience is not quite as exciting as a 20-year-old's, it is still a helluva lot better than a kick in the head.

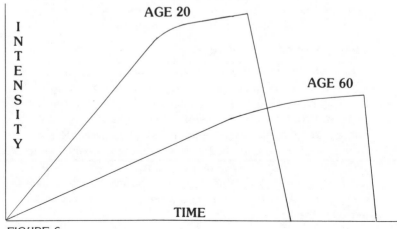

PATTERN OF SEXUAL AROUSAL (simplified)

FIGURE 6

32

We don't want to give the impression that getting older is all bad news. It has compensating factors as well. One of them is that, whether she admits it or not, the wife, too, is getting older. She has been used to having a sex drive that is less than overwhelming; as she becomes older she may find that she actually enjoys sex more than she did in her twenties. The exhausting time of pregnancies and pre-schoolers is past; she has less to distract her and more good experiences to stimulate her. This doesn't mean that she is beginning to terrorize the milkman or postman, but that sex has become more interesting, diversified and enjoyable. So she may have more real interest and enthusiasm in her fifties than she had in her twenties.

Meanwhile the husband of 50 to 60 has, we hope, learned to control the hair-trigger on his firing mechanism, has become adjusted to a more moderate drive and has become a more patient and skillful lover. He and his wife are now more evenly matched, and, potentially, more compatible. This is good news.

But the news is not all good. This change in the man from a strong rapid drive to a more moderate and slower response calls for some adjustments on the part of both husband and wife.

The first adjustment is that **both must allow him more time** — more time to get into the mood in the first place, and then more time to get into action. There are no more in-stant jack-rabbit starts. The days of burning rubber are long gone!

A retired farmer has been coming in for his annual physical examination for many years. He had always been sexually active, but when he reached his 80's he began to slow down. This was fine with his wife. But for him sex still had many rewards; so he spent much of his indoor time stalking his wife around the house. She was 20 years younger than he and much fleeter of foot; so his contacts were few. When he would finally get her cornered, she would bob and weave and side step like Muhammed Ali, and he would go crashing past her into a cupboard, and come up empty again.

He came into the office after his 82nd birthday feeling very sad. The story was this: On his 82nd birthday, they had given him a big party and after he had blown out all the candles and regained his wind, they went up to bed and his wife said to him: "Okay lover boy, you have ten minutes." This sad, old gentleman said to me: "Hell, I couldn't get my shoes off in ten minutes!" — and so there he was tugging at his socks, and it was suddenly "Game over." In this ball game, the poor old man not only had not gotten to first base, he hadn't even been able to pick up his bat. He was sad, because if this was to be only an annual event, he was not really sure that he would be around for an encore on his 83rd birthday. And so he had come, more for sympathy than advice, because the only advice one could give him was to walk around in his bare feet so he would be ready. He realized he was a little old for this barefoot boy routine. During a Canadian winter he would be getting much more frostbite than sex! So this was not a feasible alternative either.

The point of this story, in case you have somehow missed it, is that the amount of time is important.

A second adjustment is that **men, in later years, may require foreplay to become fully aroused** and ready for coitus. Again, note the male and the female becoming more alike. Foreplay for a young man is like gilding the lily (a beautiful luxury, great sport, but not necessary). Foreplay for the older man may be a necessity, and so it's important for the wife to learn the art of physical seduction. Notice, too, once again how important communication will be in this sphere with the roles reversed.

A third adjustment is that **both partners must become aware of the importance of circumstances.** Both must arrange for the most favorable time and place.

As the male libido becomes weaker, it can be damaged by many things and many circumstances; so both must learn not to expect him to function unless circumstances are reasonably good.

If demands are made on the man and circumstances are not good, they will be confronted with a new challenge — the problem of impotence.

CHAPTER 6

IMPOTENCE:
THE SPIRIT IS WILLING
BUT THE FLESH IS WEAK

The definition of male impotence is simply the inability to produce and maintain an erection long enough to get the penis into the vagina. That doesn't sound like much to ask, but sometimes it's quite a problem.

Impotence can be either **occasional** or **continuing.** Occasional impotence is something that will happen sooner or later to every man, but it occurs more often in older men and others whose sexual drive is easily affected by inhibiting factors. It should not be cause for any alarm.

Continuing impotence is a matter for more concern; it can be the result of either physical or psychological problems.

Among the **physical causes,** chronic fatigue is the most common. Some diseases produce impotence, and also some drugs. An important cause these days are the drugs used to control high blood pressure. Because these pills are sometimes needed to keep the husband alive, he is faced with a difficult choice. He can choose to go down with all of his guns blazing, without his pills; or he can choose to fade away slowly into the sunset with his pills — but living with a certain amount of misfiring of his guns. Of course, we are hoping that medical science can get this worked out so we will all be able to keep firing away until dark. Incidentally, these same drugs also have an inhibiting effect on the libido of women.

Psychological causes of impotence are sometimes obvious. This is the case where impotence is just one symptom of a generally sick husband-wife relationship. It also applies where impotence is the end result of years of unresolved sexual conflict. What seems to happen in these cases is that the man's memory bank becomes full of either bad or indifferent sexual memories; unconsciously, he decides it isn't worth it. He weighs the expected enjoyment against the ef-

35

fort and frustration involved, and he comes up with a goose egg, instead of an erection. He's turned off sexually and quite content to be impotent.

FEAR — FAILURE CYCLE

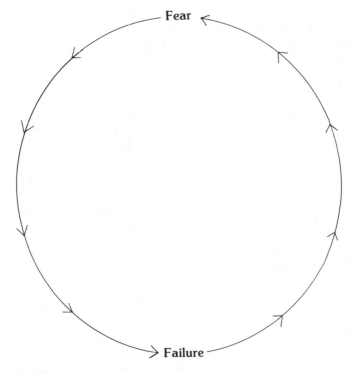

FIGURE 7

Sometimes, though, a period of impotence occurs in what seems to be a completely satisfactory marriage. The husband desires intercourse, but he finds himself incapable of producing an erection. Then, after six months or so, potency often returns as suddenly and mysteriously as it departed. In these cases, impotence seems to be the result of several minor unconscious inhibiting influences plus one last straw. All it takes to get the husband functioning again is the

36

removal of a straw or two. This can happen accidently or through the efforts of the couple to understand and improve the situation. Unless it is complicated by fear, this kind of impotence is usually temporary.

A common psychological cause of continuing impotence is the fear-failure cycle (Figure 7). This starts when the man has a failure. The reason may be quite obvious. For example, **too much to drink, or attempting intercourse too frequently.** Or it may be more puzzling. In either case the man is frightened — frightened that he has suffered permanent loss of his ability to function sexually. The next time he tries to have an erection he is too anxious to be able to function; this increases his fear, which leads to continuing failure, and so on in a vicious circle.

Wives will understand this better if they realize that failure in sexual function can be a shattering, terrifying experience for the male ego. It's a feeling, not a rational reaction. The degree and intensity of this feeling appears absurd to everyone except the poor fellow who is impotent. But to him it's very real. Failure here can produce a deep and abiding fear of repeated failure. So instead of being relaxed and joyous, sexual intimacy becomes a series of demands, a time of testing — full of fears and misgivings. Instead of an erection being an automatic reaction, it becomes a job, something he must work to produce — and he's not at all sure that he **can** produce. The more he worries, the worse it gets. The harder he tries, the softer it gets. Finally, he just lies there and spins his wheels, bites the pillow, and curses himself to sleep.

Most wives handle this situation well. They are understanding, patient and reassuring. They express confidence that things will return to normal, and in the meantime make it clear that the situation is not a big problem for them. This is fortunate, since a man in this position needs a good friend and lots of reassurance.

Occasionally, however, a wife decides that the situation calls for an all-out attempt at seducing her husband. In terms of sheer terror, this must be the equivalent of being thrown into a lion's den with your hands tied behind your

FEAR — FAILURE CYCLE SPIN-OFF

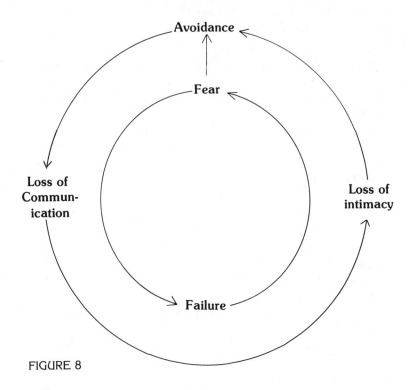

FIGURE 8

back. There's no option but to run and keep running.

If the husband can be reassured, the fear-failure cycle can be broken. If not, there is likely to be a spinoff into another destructive cycle.

Because the husband can't bear the thought of another failure, he begins to avoid his wife. Avoidance on his part then produces a loss of communication between them and, inevitably, a loss of psychological intimacy. To his wife, this loss of intimacy means rejection and she either objects or adjusts. If she doesn't object and begin asking questions she also fails to communicate her concern, and the loss of intimacy becomes further established. At this point they have become cut off from the sustaining strength of physical affection and psychological closeness. They have become two lonely individuals instead of one close couple. Sex, instead of being a unifying and healing influence in their lives, has become a divisive and destructive force.

Most couples in good marriages can cope if they can understand the mechanics of this spin off — that the husband has chosen to avoid his wife only because avoidance is preferable to another unbearable defeat. If they can communicate with trust, understanding and acceptance, psychological intimacy can be restored. They will usually find that a very minor event or influence began this whole chain of failures — and with recognition of the source of the problem will usually come release from the problem.

Even when potency can't be completely restored (where drugs or illness are factors, for example), couples can learn to live with impotence as they learn to live with other inconvenient facts of life; it need not be something that has any power to undermine their love.

It is very important, at all ages, not to worry about, nor concentrate on performance, scores or batting averages, but to zero in more on physical affection, psychological closeness and oneness. These will last forever. These are what we can have always and share always — long after our last orgasm is only a faint memory. They will produce a growing, deepening and enriching physical and emotional relationship right up to the very ends of our lives.

A dear, little fragile old couple in their late 70's comes into the office periodically for tune-ups. He is obviously too crocked up for much sex, but they both act as though they are on their first date. Their relationship obviously is not suffering because of the lack of sex. Their love is very much alive. And because it is a mutual love, each is helping the other's love to grow forever. Though they may not be able even to remember when he had his last erection, they are not missing a thing, because they have this real love in common — a love that is strong and healthy and still growing. This is what is of the ultimate importance. This is what marriage should be all about.

CHAPTER 7

SO WHAT'S THE ANSWER?

"Doesn't it seem that God made a mistake when He made men and women so different?" We were once asked this by a young man, a discouraged veteran of seven years of marriage. It's a reasonable question. If automatic and effortless sexual compatibility was what the Almighty had in mind, it does seem that He blew it!

But we believe that He intends the experience of marriage and parenthood to be (for most of us) the principal means by which we are challenged to grow in love. If sexual compatibility was pre-arranged by biological programming, there would be little in our sexual interaction to stimulate change. As it is, we encounter conflict, crisis and pain. We can react with cynicism and despair, and take up arms in "the battle of the sexes." Or we can grow in wisdom and in love, building a relationship more rich and complex than anything we could imagine as newlyweds.

Since **the key to sexual harmony in marriage is love,** we'll take "time out" at this point in our examination of marital sexuality to take a closer look at this key. What is this love on which everything depends?

When we use the word love in this context, we have in mind the Christian concept of love as "agape," "caritas," "benevolentia." What psychologists call "mature love" closely resembles this Christian understanding of love.

41

There are some things this kind of love **is not** (but with which it may be confused). It is not infatuation, or "falling in love." It is not the same as being loved — or the good feelings we have when we are loved. It is not sexual desire, or sexual union; nor is it the same as need — the kind of dependency attachment a two-year-old has to his mother. Nor does loving someone mean indulging or "spoiling" him any more than self-love implies self-indulgence. The fact that some of these elements are present in a relationship does not mean that love is absent; love normally co-exists with many of them. But to understand the nature of love itself, we must look farther.

We read in the New Testament that "God is love." No wonder we find it impossible to capture love in neat definitions and tidy explanations. Yet this doesn't mean that we can know nothing about it. Drawing on the combined insights of Christian tradition and psychology, we can find much that is helpful in giving direction to our efforts to grow in love.

Christian tradition has described love as **the movement of our being toward God.** "Our hearts are made for thee, Lord, and they are restless 'til they rest in thee." Just as we meet the artist in his painting, the writer in his book, so we meet God in His creation — in all the things, and especially in all the persons that He has made. We are moved to love persons, and even the material world, because they reflect something of the beauty and goodness of God for whom we were made. Christian tradition also tells us that our love is **a reflection of God's own nature in us.** God is love, and it is, above all, in our capacity to live in loving relationship with others that we are made in His image. These descriptions of love are encouraging because they tell us that **it is our nature to love.** The requirements of love are therefore not some foreign law that we impose on ourselves because we are told that we should. Rather, they are clues to our own identity and fulfillment. We have difficulties in love, not because love is foreign to us, but because sin has mixed us up. As a result, we often are inclined to choose a lesser good at the expense of a greater one usually because the rewards of the lesser good are more obvious and immediate. It is because of this tendency — not because love is unnatural for us — that we need to use our heads and to exercise self-discipline if we are to progress in love.

Another helpful description of love comes from St. Thomas. "To love someone," he tells us, "is to will his highest good." He explains further that this "highest good" is to become the person God created him to be. We have found this a very useful way of looking at love. For one thing, it makes it easy to understand both how and why we are to love ourselves. For another, it provides the basis for distinguishing between loving others and indulging or "spoiling" them, and for distinguishing between self-love and selfishness. Love requires that we seek God's will for those we love, including ourselves, even at the cost of some immediate disappointment and frustration.

If we want to grow in love, it is useful to have in mind a clear picture of the main characteristics of mature love. For that reason, we're going to review these characteristics briefly. This will provide us with clear guidelines as we attempt to apply these principles of love in our sexual interaction.

I. Mature love is a faculty and an art.

Like other faculties (powers, personal qualities), love can be cultivated and developed; like other arts, it can be learned and improved upon with dedicated practice.

It follows then that finding love is not a matter of chance; it's not something we fall into if we're lucky, but miss out on if we're not. It also follows that the problem in love is not in **finding** the right person but in **becoming** the right person — one who is capable of loving. If one can't play the guitar, changing guitars won't help. Whether or not our lives are rich in love is to a large extent up to us, although the important "others" in our lives can certainly help or hinder us.

II. Mature love is other-centered

It is normal for the young child to see others, to use them, to value them, in terms of "How do they affect me?" Learning to love maturely means growing beyond this **self-**

centered way of relating to others, and becoming instead **other-centered.** Mature love unlocks the prison of self; it makes it possible for us to enter into the world of others, to live in and for them and not just for ourselves.

There's no conflict between this other-centered movement of love and self-love. As Eric Fromm has observed, this other-centered thrust of love "is the answer to the deepest need of man — the need to overcome his separateness, to leave the prison of his aloneness." The Gospel expresses the same truth when it tells us that only the man who is willing to lose his life will save it.

This other-centered quality of mature love manifests itself in many ways:

Respect — Our English word "respect" comes from the Latin word which means "to look at." When we respect, we see the other as he really is, not in terms of our own needs and purposes. We will not try to violate his freedom to be himself, by trying to dominate, to use, or to manipulate him.

Unconditional acceptance — To love maturely is to love people **as they are.** "Love" that is conditional on good behavior is love of good behavior, not love of the person.

Loving unconditionally doesn't mean being a door-mat. We can say, "No" to unreasonable demands or behavior without withdrawing our love. Nor does unconditional love make us blind to the faults or indifferent to the growth of those we love. We can still encourage them to grow — but in their own way, and for their own sake, and in fidelity to themselves. Meanwhile, we love them as they are today — warts and all — giving them space and time to grow according to their own timetable.

Knowledge and Understanding — When we love unconditionally, we create a climate in which the other feels safe in letting down his defenses and opening himself freely to us. When this happens, the other-centered movement of love will carry us into the other's world, where we can think his thoughts, feel his feelings, need his needs, dream his dreams. So mature love leads, not just to a surface knowledge **about** a person, but to a deep knowing and understanding from within.

Communication — Communication is the essential bridge which makes it possible for us to enter into the world of others and to receive them into ours. It takes dedicated effort to build and maintain this bridge. Fortunately, married couples today have many good opportunities to grow in this vital dimension of love. If our love is other-centered, we will take advantage of these opportunities.

Giving — Eric Fromm describes love as "an active power in man that expresses itself above all in the action of giving." Not all giving is a sign of love, however. To be an expression of love, our giving must meet certain conditions. There must be no strings attached. Otherwise we are trading, not giving. It must be a cheerful and a joyful giving — never a giving-up, or a giving-in. It must be above all a giving of self (not just things, or services). And it must be a response to the other's real needs — a giving not of what it makes us feel good to give, but of what the other needs to receive. The giving of love is therefore marked by **responsibility** and **care.**

III. Mature love seeks union with integrity

It is the nature of love to seek union. That's why we get married. But love requires that there be at the same time a mutual commitment to our continued wholeness and growth as individuals. The result is likely to be a complicated and lively relationship — one in which there is tension and conflict. When there is no conflict in a marriage, we can suspect either a lack of unity (husband and wife leading separate lives) or the domination of one partner by the other.

IV. Mature love is honest and real

People are sometimes under the impression that love requires them to wear a mask — to smile sweetly and be kind and agreeable even when what is in their hearts is icy indifference or the urge to kill. This results in hypocrites not lovers.

Love does require that we try to behave ourselves. (That

45

urge to kill should be suppressed!) But the basic attitudes of love — respect, unconditional acceptance, the will to know and understand, communication, responsibility, care, faith — these must be real and can be real, even in the midst of conflicts and negative feelings. Love will not cover up problems with play-acting, but bring them out into the open where they can be dealt with realistically and honestly.

V. Mature love has its roots in faith

Love has the courage to be honest because it is rooted in faith. We have faith in those we love — we're sure about the core of their personalities, their essential goodness, their love for us. This is only possible if we have faith in ourselves — in our own worth, our own power to love — and to call forth love in others. This presupposes faith in love itself, and, in the case of married love, faith in marriage; in the possibility that love can be faithful and grow for a lifetime, in spite of the inevitable frustrations and disappointments. For the Christian, all these dimensions of faith are expressions of one faith — faith in the God revealed to us by Jesus. The Father's goodness is the guarantee of the essential goodness of everything and everyone that He has made.

It is this faith that makes it possible for love to put down deep roots in the will, in something more solid and constant than emotion. And it is this faith that gives us the hope we need to work at resolving conflicts, instead of giving in to despair and cynicism.

Obviously, these characteristics of love represent an ideal. In practice, we all fall far short of this ideal. If we react to this with discouragement and guilt, we are missing the point. Learning to love is like learning to walk — only it takes a lot longer. The significant thing is not that we often fail, but that we sometimes succeed. If we keep trying and making even a little progress, we have reason to congratulate ourselves and each other. The ideal isn't there to make us feel guilty, but to give support and direction to our efforts.

In addition to these characteristics of love, there are a few other principles or **"facts of love"** that we need to keep in mind in our sexual interaction — and indeed in our marriage generally. They are of such practical importance that they deserve a prominent place on our list of "things we must not forget."

The first of these important facts of love is that **the basis of all love is self-love.** I must love myself before I can love others. It follows then that anything a wife does that increases her husband's self-esteem at the same time increases his capacity to love her. Anything a husband does that diminishes his wife's self-esteem will reduce her capacity to love him. The harder husband and wife work at building each other's self-esteem, the more their love for each other will flourish. What a tragedy, then, when a marriage is full of belittling and fault-finding. Every blow at a partner's self-esteem weakens the foundation of love for his or her spouse.

Which brings us to a second fact of love — **we learn to love by being loved.** It is by letting his wife know that he finds her lovable that a husband helps her to love herself; this in turn helps her to love him more. The more exuberant and enthusiastic his love for her, the more her love for him will be nourished.

Still another fact — **people tend to become what we tell them they are.** The wife who keeps up a nagging refrain of "You don't love me" has a good chance of convincing her husband that she's right. The husband who labels his wife "lazy" or "frigid" will probably end up with a wife who fits his description. To put it another way — **"we grow only for people who believe in us, who trust us, who love us."** It is, above all, by having faith in each other — and communicating this faith — that we stimulate each other's growth.

Love doesn't keep score. This is a fortunate fact of love, because any marriage in which husband and wife are only prepared to give 50% is doomed. For one thing, his version of 50% is unlikely to match her version. For another, there'll be days when one or the other will have trouble coming up with 2%! Only if both try to give all they are capable of giving can they hope, between them, to scrape up enough generosity to see them through the rough times.

Along the same lines, marriage has been compared to a joint bank account. If both partners are only interested in

47

making withdrawals, there'll be nothing in it for either. If, instead, they concentrate on putting as much as they can into it, there'll probably be enough to satisfy all their needs.

A sad fact of love is that **love can die in a climate of chronic indifference and neglect.** Ideally, this shouldn't be true. Perfect love continues to love indefinitely, even in the face of brutal rejection. This is the way God loves, of course, but there aren't many humans who can manage it. For most of us, there's a limit to how much pain we can absorb before something deep inside us says, "No more" — and we stop caring. We see this in marriages, where, after years of neglect and rejection, a long-suffering spouse finally decides to call it quits. Suddenly, the negligent spouse is full of interest and plans for working at the relationship, but it's too late. The partner has passed beyond both love and hate to indifference. As Rhett Butler put it, in the novel *Gone With The Wind* — "Frankly, my dear, I don't give a damn!"

It behooves us, then, not to coast, depending on a generous partner to pick up the slack indefinitely.

A final important fact of love is that **love is contagious.** So are other attitudes, like selfishness, and indifference. Love in one spouse calls forth love in the other; selfishness in one spouse calls forth selfishness in the other. For this reason, the struggle to grow in love in marriage is very much a team effort; we usually sink or swim together.

There are exceptions, of course. Some people, during their vulnerable childhood years, have received fatal wounds to their capacity to trust and to love. Trying to call forth love in these people is the equivalent of trying to raise the dead. It is beyond the power of the most generous and steadfast of human loves.

But in most marriages, the partners have a potential for both love and selfishness. They can go either way — and so can the marriage; it can become a heaven or a hell depending on whether the partners bring out the best or the worst in themselves and each other. Because attitudes are contagious, the end result is usually **mutual** — whether mutual indifference, mutual hatred, or mutual love. Husbands and wives usually end up deserving each other.

CHAPTER 8

THE ART OF SEDUCTION

Now that we have reviewed some of the principles of love, we are ready to consider some of the ways in which we are challenged to put these principles into practice in our sexual interaction.

For most couples, the first challenge is likely to be to the young husband; he must learn very early that he can never stop courting and wooing his wife. Sometimes a young man makes the mistake of assuming that, once he marries the girl, she will be available for coitus and respond happily to it any old time, under any old conditions, and without any preparation. But most women are not made that way, and can't force themselves to be that way, no matter how much they love their husbands. They might decide in their heads that they will try; but their feelings and bodies just won't cooperate. So if a husband wants a happy wife, and a warm sexual partner, he has to become an expert in the art of seduction — of preparing his wife first emotionally, and then physically, for coitus.

Sooner or later, wives too should learn the art of seduction. Many tend to give up on this in the honeymoon stage; they figure that they have all the action they can handle without playing the siren. But as a man becomes older, he becomes more of a gourmet and a connoisseur in this relationship. The quality of lovemaking becomes more important as the quantity becomes less so. It is important that wives respond to this change — that they accept more responsibility for keeping this relationship fresh and exciting by applying a bit more imagination and effort to it.

Even in the earlier years it is to be hoped that there will be times when the wife takes the initiative; it's a bit hard on the husband's morale otherwise. And right from the beginning in some marriages it will be the wife who usually takes the initiative. In this case she will be the first one who needs to learn the art of seduction.

49

We will be talking in terms of the more common situation, that in which the young husband must learn the art of seduction first. However, we invite you to be aware that sometimes the roles will be reversed. If that is the way it is with you, just reverse things as we go along. What we will be saying applies just as much when the wife takes the initiative. The principles of the art of seduction are the same, whether it is the husband or the wife who is practicing the art.

A woman's love and her subsequent sexual response are not something that a husband can take for granted. It is not something that the man can demand or something that the wife can force. It is something that has to be earned continually and won more or less repeatedly.

During the honeymoon phase, a man can expect a certain amount of spontaneous activity. But this activity can't stand alone and will not survive by itself. Nor is there a lifetime guarantee on it. So if a wife's response and her desire peter out, a husband will be in trouble. There is not even a one-year warranty on the moving parts! Husbands can't return the unused portion or get their money back. Society still frowns on trade-ins and pinch hitters. So the options are not nearly as many as one would like to think. This means that husbands have to keep their wits about them because a wife with a dead battery is not much fun.

To be a successful lover, a man must function intelligently in two different spheres — the spheres of psychological seduction and physical seduction. (When we refer to the need for husbands to function intelligently, we realize that this puts many wives behind the eightball immediately.) Naturally psychological seduction comes first. In the early days of marriage, there may not be much of a problem; but it can become one before long. It's amazing to find out how many men simply cannot believe that psychological seduction is necessary every time. They seem to say, "She should be able to remember the good times, and be anxious for a re-run. She had a ball New Year's eve. Why do I have to keep bringing her back from the dead every time?" But this is the way the good Lord designed most women. We are sure it is to help men grow out of the "naked ape" stage — to learn to be gentle, thoughtful, understanding and wise. None of these attributes are instinctive to Naked Apes.

There are several elements necessary for psychological seduction. In the early months of marriage or in an ideal marriage, most of these elements may be present all of the time; so the wife is psychologically prepared for coitus most of the time. But this can be a trap for a lazy or careless husband who then assumes that she will be "hot to trot" forever. He gets sloppy and before long finds himself in trouble.

The first element is that there be **a climate of love** for the woman. When I talk about a climate, I mean consistency, not a hot and cold relationship, not a bouquet one day and a belt in the mouth the next — but an abiding love, so that she always knows where she stands.

In this love there must be provision for her instinctive love needs and her special human needs. With the instinctive love needs mentioned earlier, she has to feel precious, secure, valued and know that she comes first in his life. The special human needs are for friendship, affection and romance. She must know that she is his best friend, not like a spare on a bowling team, or someone he calls on when there is no one else interesting around, but the one he would prefer to be with all the time if he had his choice. So, if he can provide for these needs, and produce this climate, then from the point of view of seduction he should be sitting pretty (unless she has stomach flu or a slipped disc which will put her on the shelf for a few days).

If this climate exists, then there is the possibility of the second element which we call an **"Emotional Bridge."** This is a bridge of psychological closeness which is a prerequisite for physical closeness.

This bridge is not necessarily present just because the wife is in a good marriage. We see this frequently when a husband has to leave town for three or four months. When he comes home, he finds, not a sexually-aroused wife, but a semi-stranger, who can't get herself untracked and can't really react to him in a physical way, even though she is happy with her marriage overall. They will have to re-establish psychological closeness before she is ready for physical closeness. The husband, too, may find that the bridge that was in great shape on Tuesday night is a total disaster Wednesday afternoon when he comes home from work and finds his wife trying to unplug the toilet. It is pretty hard to get psychologically close to anyone who's up to their elbows in cold toilet water!

But when the bridge is there, it is a natural crossover from everyday feelings of contentment, warmth and satisfaction to feelings of erotic excitement when the situation is right. A young man may question the need for this bridge. He thinks "I can make it in one jump. I don't need a bridge." This may be quite true for a young man, because he can function without this bridge of psychological closeness. But his wife cannot, and he has to remember that. In the absence of this bridge — and even worse, in the opposite hostile environment of coldness, indifference, bitterness and unresolved problems — any smooth crossover is really impossible.

The results often end up in emergency wards where these guys come in to get their heads patched up. The story is usually pretty much the same. During the week, he has not spoken to his wife except to snarl at her. On Friday night he gets looped in the pub, comes home and thinks he is the world's greatest lover. He makes a pass at her and she recognizes it for what it is — just a demand for services. Then she hits him with whatever she happens to have in her hand.

In his approach to her — and she realizes this — there is no tenderness, no warmth. There is no excitement, no awe — just an appetite he has and wants satisfied. She realizes that this approach is no more romantic and no more tender than if he came home, opened the refrigerator door and took out a hunk of garlic sausage. She is insulted because she is being treated as a thing and not as a person — so she hits him again!

A third element that is necessary is **wisdom in selecting or choosing or arranging the right time and the right place.**

Men talk a lot about how easily women are distracted from erotic things. And God knows that this is often true. A fellow told me that his wife once said, "Hold it! I think the phone is going to ring!" It's hard to compete with that.

But even assuming that this is often true, it's more realistic and practical for men to realize that a woman sometimes does have things on her mind. From her point of view, it's her husband's sexual advances that are distracting. The things from which he is distracting her may be "heavy" things like the Johnny Carson show or sorting socks or doing dishes. Certainly, a man would not require too much coaxing to turn his back on this sort of thing. To him, it would be no contest at all. But to her, the importance and urgency of sex are not nearly so obvious and the man is often regarded primarily as a nuisance. A man's urgency is often a baffling thing for a woman. Her reaction may be "Well sure! But why this minute? What's wrong with Tuesday?" The husband is not sure he can last another half hour and she is talking about Tuesday.

Another element that you do not hear much about but that is extremely important is **the wife's memories of previous sexual experiences.** These memories become more important as the years go by. Her memory bank gets filled up with good memories and bad memories, of times when they've had a ball and times when they've dropped the ball. So **it is vital that there be a big store of happy sexual memories in a wife's memory bank,** when she first sees that glint in her husband's eye. Otherwise, she will say to herself, "My God, I have to think of something fast." And husbands all know how fast they can think when they are trying to get out of corners. A woman avoiding an undesired sexual encounter can make a coyote appear accident-prone by comparison.

A fifth element is that the wife must know that his attentions at this time are **a personal experience between the two of them.** She must know that she is someone unique and special in his life, that this is the reason for the action — not because he is overdue by ten days and she is finally within arm's reach. She has to realize that his attentions and caresses are not just a mechanical countdown to coitus. This isn't an impersonal, mechanical thing like greasing the skids before you launch a ship. So if she asks herself, "Am I really alive, exciting, interesting and lovable? Is this why he wants me?" and if she can truthfully answer, "Yes," then she is off and running. She can then say to herself, "I am lovable and I'm loved." Suddenly, the dishes — even her favorite TV program, especially if it's a re-run — don't seem so important to her. Sometimes she may even make the first move herself — but don't hold your breath waiting for this.

So if the psychological seduction has been successful, and we can assume that you both have the time and energy, and if it is not 4 a.m. in the morning by this time, then a man can go on to **physical seduction** and foreplay.

Foreplay has been defined as the artful stimulation of the erogenous zones. Foreplay is something that has to be learned by trial and error, practice and experience. From day one, it requires cooperation, intelligence, patience and honesty — and certainly a sense of humor to get out of tight corners.

Many men and women think that foreplay is sort of a nuisance for men, an unavoidable delay. Some men delay as little as possible; they are in a hurry to get on to the main event — the big ten-rounder! This haste makes the woman feel inadequate and under a lot of pressure, especially if she feels her spouse has a stop watch going on her. She already has enough problems without this.

The first time Mike ever heard of the existence of foreplay was during World War II as an innocent sailor.

A friend of his had a real good thing going with a girl ashore. His problem, as he related it to Mike, was that she required a half-hour of foreplay before she was ready for coitus.

This presented him with a big problem because shore leave was limited and he was an alcoholic. He felt that if he could cut this unnecessary half-hour of foreplay down to ten minutes, this would leave him with twenty minutes, during which time he could drink a whole bottle of rum and be really sick by the time he got back to the ship.

With these ends in mind he bought a sex manual and brought it back to the ship for serious study. When he came to the strange word "clitoris" he came to Mike for help. At that time Mike didn't know a clitoris from a left-handed monkey wrench! But he knew how to pronounce it and his friend knew where to find it, so they became the instant experts of the North Atlantic. Mike used to challenge him — "I can pronounce anything you can find!"

Foreplay should not be a nuisance as it was for Mike's friend — something to be rushed through quickly to get on to enjoyable things. It should not be considered a "labor of love." No one ever calls it "forework" — it is called play, and should be considered as play, and as fun.

It always amazes us how much time and ingenuity a man will spend on foreplay in the back seat of a car before he is married, and how quickly he forgets and starts taking short cuts after he is married. Inevitably their sex life becomes dull, unexciting and lifeless for his wife.

Foreplay should satisfy the man's own needs for affection, closeness, romance and for variety in erotic expression. It should be an outlet for his initiative and imagination, his way of providing an emotional as well as a physical experience for the two of them.

The **erogenous zones** are defined as those parts of the body surfaces which, when stimulated in the right way, will produce sexual excitement and sexual desire. In general, the erogenous zones can be divided into the mildly, strongly and the intensely erogenous zones. The mildly erogenous zones are all of the skin surfaces. That is why just holding hands is a mildly erogenous exercise.

The strongly erogenous zones include the lips, breasts (especially the nipples), inner thighs, buttocks and the lower abdominal area. These are standard on all models. Some women have individual variations which usually have to be searched out. Some women will go off into space if the man nibbles on an earlobe; other women will think they are tangled up with a cannibal. If a husband tries this and his wife gets up and gets him a carrot, he'll know this isn't for her.

INTENSELY EROGENOUS ZONES

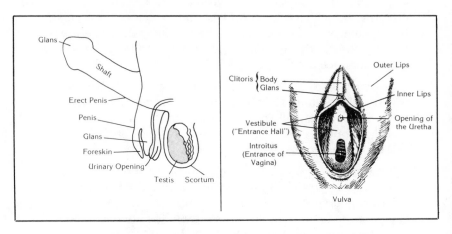

**MALE
REPRODUCTIVE ORGANS**

**FEMALE EXTERNAL
GENITAL ORGANS**

FIGURE 9

The intensely erogenous zones — otherwise known as the external sex organs — are sketched in Figure 9. On the right is a view of the intensely erogenous zones in the female. You will note that the inner lips of the vagina enclose the entrance to the vagina and the **vestibule** (the very sensitive area between the vaginal entrance and the clitoris). These lips come together at the top, enfolding the clitoris. The **clitoris** has two parts — the hidden **body,** and the **glans —** just peeking out.

On the left we have a side view of the intensely erogenous zones in the male. Enclosed in the scrotum are the testes. The **penis** like the clitoris, has two parts — the **shaft** of the penis, and the **glans,** or head.

Probably none of this comes as a surprise to most of you.

56

However, you may not be aware that the tissue and the nerve supply in the shaft of the penis is the same as the tissue and the nerve supply in the inner lips of the vagina; and the tissue and the nerve supply in the glans (or head) of the penis is the same as the tissue and the nerve supply in the glans of the clitoris. This gives some idea of the similarities between men and women and therefore of what they are able to do for one another in the way of erotic stimulation. Women, however, have an "extra." The vestibule is an extremely sensitive and erogenous area; there is nothing external that corresponds to it in the male.

But the most important erogenous zone of all is the brain. A cynic was once heard to remark — "That's an awfully small target!" But the brain is really the master switch for erotic function. It's a sort of rheostat, and until it is fully turned on the woman will be full of short circuits. It is important for women to know that husbands, too, have a master switch. Many young brides think their husbands are stuck in the "on" position. But husbands too have a rheostat; it just gets turned on very quickly. As they get older, it gets turned on more slowly and, finally, may even start to slip a bit.

Remember, the word erogenous refers only to the **potential** of an area. There are no guarantees here. Stimulation of these areas is not necessarily going to produce an erotic response. It will occur only if the husband uses the right kind of stimulation (light touch) and only if the wife has reached the right psychological state, that is, if she is feeling right in her mind and heart toward her husband and her body is wanting him. So a certain level of desire has to be present before the strongly and intensely erogenous zones will actually respond in an erotic way.

If there is no desire, or if the level of desire is not high enough (if the man is going too far, too fast), then stimulating these zones will be ineffective or worse; it may actually be painful. For instance, if the man has just read about the clitoris and zooms in on it like a homing pigeon, it will be physically unpleasant and even painful for the woman, because there has been no physical preparation. Without proper lubrication, she is just not ready. Caressing

the clitoris like this would be quite similar to the wife thinking she would turn her husband on if she caressed his
eyeball. You can imagine how long he'd keep up a head of
steam if she kept sticking her thumb in his eye! So you can
see that even under the best psychological conditions, and
after the husband has knocked himself out with the full
gamut of psychological seduction, unless that master switch
is almost fully turned on when he reaches those intensely
erogenous zones, her circuit breaker will cut out. Her fuses
will blow and they will be left in the cold and in the dark.
She will be cold again and he will be in the dark still. And
that is not progress.

PATTERN OF AROUSAL

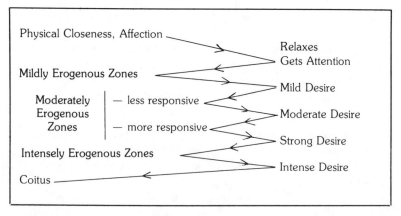

FIGURE 10

So there is a general pattern of arousal to be followed
which is roughly illustrated in Figure 10. This may seem artificial and mechanical at first. But it is the pattern, whether
you recognize it or not, that is actually followed. Often the
wife will be in the state of moderate desire, or even strong
desire, before her husband even thinks about it. This is
perfectly normal, but possible only because she has been living in this climate of warmth and love and has already passed through the initial earlier stages by herself.

In this pattern you first of all have physical closeness and affection — the climate of love that we referred to earlier. This climate is necessary before a woman can be relaxed, and she must be relaxed before there is any point in trying to get her attention. Have you ever reached for your wife and she leaped like a scalded cat? If you were smart you realized that — as they say in the Bible — your time had not yet come. But, if you have her attention, then caressing the mildly erogenous zones may produce a mild desire. By the time you have worked your way up to her naked upper arm, she may not be quite ready to stop watching TV, but you can usually get in a few good licks during the commercial. This mild desire then prepares the less responsive of the moderately erogenous zones to react when caressed and pro- duce a moderate desire. At this point, she might even be willing to butt her cigarette, but as somebody once said, "If she butts her cigarette in your hand, you know you are do- ing something wrong." This moderate desire activates the more responsive of the moderately erogenous zones. When they are stimulated, they produce a strong desire that prepares the intensely erogenous zones. It is at this point — and not until this point — that stimulating the intensely erogenous zones will produce an intense desire for coitus.

Foreplay is an art, something that has to be learned. Because it is an art, it **involves both style and timing.** When we talk about style we have in mind using imagination to provide variety and surprise, and keeping out of ruts and routine as much as possible. Foreplay should also involve sensitivity and lightness of touch. The rule here is: the more sensitive the area, the lighter the touch must be.

All this may sound perfectly obvious. But a man may make the mistake of thinking that his enthusiasm is a con- tagious thing, and the more boisterous and athletic he becomes, the more excited his wife will become. So the poor girl comes to the next morning, covered with bruises and thumbprints and hickeys, with or without a cracked rib, and as she regains consciousness, she doesn't remember if she got hit by a Mack truck or mauled by a grizzly bear. Then she looks at the guy with the big dumb smile on his face and remembers that he had a ball, but she is not sure how long she can survive this kind of entertainment nor does she know how fast she can heal. So that is not a recommended technique.

Timing means a gradual arousal, with an unhurried approach. If you have to keep checking your watch, you had better forget it. If you are in the car pool and you are up and down like a yo-yo every time you hear a car coming down the street, you had better take a raincheck. You will be back that night anyhow. There is really no point in panicking.

The key, again, is for the wife's desire to keep one step ahead of her husband's caresses. So the real guide has to be the wife's responses and reactions. It is her responsibility to learn to communicate her reactions verbally and non-verbally. She should communicate her enjoyment or discomfort, whether he is going too fast or is rough or applying too much pressure, or should move his hand just a little to the right. These are fairly simple pieces of information to pass back and forth. But if all is going well and there is nothing to say, she can at least purr and he will catch on very quickly.

Some wives only communicate in this area if something is going wrong. The wife will suddenly yell, "Ouch, damn it! You've done it again!" He doesn't even know what he did the first time. It is pretty tough for him to know what is going on if that is all the information she passes on to him. So any experimentation will be a pretty frightening thing to him.

In all areas of life, if they are able to communicate, husband and wife teach one another. In this particular area, she is really the teacher, and so it is important for her to remember that, basically, this student of hers is not too bright. A certain percentage of goofs is par for the course in the early years. The situation is like that of a kid who is almost toilet trained. Things may go along great for a couple of weeks and then suddenly there is this great mess on the floor — and you realize he is not yet fully trained. We don't expect the husband to make a mess on the carpet, but he is not always going to be a winner either. So the wife must be prepared to be both gracious and understanding with his inevitable miscalculations.

60

A common error that men make is in misinterpreting the woman's present state of arousal. A classical example of this is the situation when the young wife gets a very bad head cold. When lovemaking begins and they get down to some prolonged kissing, her breathing becomes labored very quickly. In all likelihood, his breathing is also becoming labored and this is when he starts to misinterpret.

He thinks they are going neck and neck down the home stretch, whereas, in fact, she is merely trying her damnedest to stay alive. What she needs more than sex, at this time, are nose drops. He is mistaking air hunger for passion. He is down at the bottom of that pattern of arousal chart (Figure 10), foaming a bit at the mouth, and heading for home, while she is still up at the top of the chart, desperately trying to get relaxed — and get oxygen — and it is no wonder they head into a confused situation.

The wife too, must learn to participate in love-making and show some enthusiasm for it, because nothing can destroy a man's initiative faster than repeatedly having to make love to someone who just lies there like some dead thing that got washed up on the beach. If he has to shake her wrist every once in awhile to check for rigor mortis, or if the only sign of life is an occasional gasp he will be tempted to get her an iron lung, and take off for more lively pastures.

Foreplay, then, **should be a two-way street,** with both feeling free to do what comes naturally to them and what gives pleasure to both of them. With a little luck, the wife will reach the stage of intense desire and be willing and eager to go on to coitus. As a general rule, she should be the one to decide when to begin coitus. This should be obvious to all husbands, but somehow it seems to elude many of them.

Remember, all the positions, all the caresses, contortions and techniques that can be devised, are neither good nor bad in themselves — they are neutral. They can all become good if they are **welcomed** by the partner; they can all become bad if they are **forced** on the partner.

We think it is important to stress this, because, with the

almost infinite number of how-to-do-it books available, ranging from kooky to queer to frankly kinky, an eager husband can be easily confused. So, husbands, remember — what turns your crank may turn her stomach. Don't assume. Don't be surprised. Don't try to train her to have a stouter stomach. These are tricks that just don't appeal to her; so lay off. This advice of course, applies also to wives of an adventurous nature.

Foreplay, in general, should be looked on as fun and as play — as a way of saying something special to someone special. With this approach, we will be sensitive to the needs, the wants and the desires of our partners. Then, we will both be eager to go on and experiment, to give extra depth and variety to our love-making.

There will be times when the husband reaches orgasm ahead of schedule and is eventually unable to continue coitus even though his wife has not reached orgasm. It comes as a surprise to not a few husbands to find that the loving response to this situation is not to lie there and pant, nor to light a cigarette and offer her a puff but to find out if she is content as is, or if she requires an orgasm to complete her evening. If the latter is her answer, he should continue with afterplay with any stimulation she needs. There is no way in which more brownie points can be accumulated with such ease and such enjoyment.

After the love-making, there is a period called the **"afterglow."** Some husbands, for some strange reason, after both have reached orgasm, just stop dead in their tracks, and have no further contact with their wives at all. Many even appear to feel indifferent to their wives. It is normal in the animal kingdom for the stallion to feel indifferent about the mare after mating. All he is really interested in at this stage is a big drink of water and a gallon of oats. This is normal for a horse. But it is not normal behavior for a husband. He may be thirsty but oats are out.

This behavior is very unsettling for the wife because if affection is suddenly turned off like a tap, and he seems to be either indifferent to her or to be turned in upon himself and ignoring her and her needs, her instinctive love needs are again threatened, her instinctive love source is being weakened and she begins to feel unloved, and used and abused. She is suddenly insecure and very vulnerable. Sexual intercourse, for her, has become something to be feared and avoided because it has this unhappy ending.

This period of afterglow, then, need not be any more exciting than just lying in each other's arms and catching one's breath. Couples may or may not even feel like talking. The important thing about it is that it is a time of peace and contentment — a time when both can feel secure, safe and above all sure — sure of each other's love, sure that it can grow even more (that it is just starting), sure of the permanency of love. In today's world, there are very few places and very few times where we can feel this sure about anything and this is one reason why we should really use this time to the fullest.

We don't want to leave the impression that making sexual intercourse mutually fulfilling is all the husband's responsibility. The wife has an active part to play as well. It is up to her to make sure there is a place in her life for making love. When women fill every day with 25 hours worth of other activities, the wisest husband can't find a right time or place. It is also up to her to exercise self-discipline — to do her best to put distraction out of her mind and to get on the same wavelength as her husband. We have already stressed the importance of both communication and active participation on her part. And, of course, foreplay should not be a one-way street; it should be a mutual giving and receiving of both partners, one to the other. We have stressed the wife's needs and responses in foreplay because this is an area of practical difficulty for many couples.

We remind you again that it is important that a wife, too, learn the art of seduction, since it is to be hoped that there will be times when she will take the initiative. In some marriages it is usually the wife who takes the initiative. When she does so, all the same principles apply — such things as, a climate of love for the husband, wisdom in selecting the right time and place, and letting her husband's responses be her guide.

CHAPTER 9
WHEN SEXUAL APPETITES DIFFER

Very few couples find that they are a perfect match when it comes to sexual interest and energy. Sometimes it's the wife who has the heartier sexual appetite; this becomes more likely as the couple gets older, but some start out this way. More often though, especially in the first 20 or so years of marriage, it's the wife who can't keep up with her husband in this department. We've already considered some of the biological influences responsible for this.

It's been suggested that there is often a ratio of about two to one — the young husband desiring and being capable of a full response about twice as often as his wife. Someone else has suggested that it's not a matter of quantity; rather it's because men and women march to different drummers when it comes to sexual desire.

FEMALE DESIRE

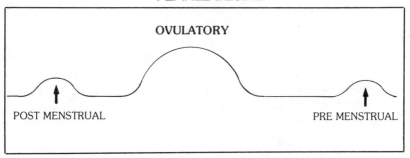

FIGURE 11

In Figure 11, we see the woman's desire fluctuating, depending on where she is in her menstrual cycle. There's a little flurry of interest after the menstrual period, lots of interest around the time of ovulation, and then another little blip of interest prior to the next period.

FEMALE AND MALE DESIRE

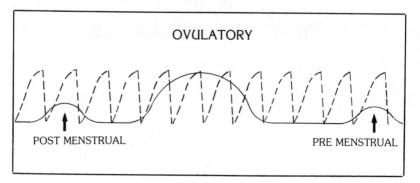

FEMALE DESIRE _____

MALE DESIRE (intercourse occurring about every 48 hours)__ __ __

FIGURE 12

Superimposed on this, in Figure 12, we see her young husband's desire bubbling along merrily in an every 48-hour pattern. Looking at an arrangement like this, it really requires an act of faith to believe that it was made in heaven.

In Figure 12, it is assumed that intercourse is occurring every 48 hours. If intercourse never occurs, we get the situation illustrated in Figure 13; the husband's desire goes up and gets stuck up there.

This is the wife who confides in hushed tones that her husband is a "sex maniac!" Every time she slows down for a turn he leaps out at her from behind doors or furniture. It comes as quite a surprise to this lady to realize that if they have intercourse once in a while, his sex mania clears up very nicely — at least for the time being!

66

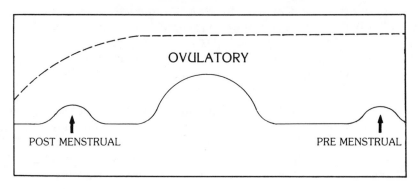

NO INTERCOURSE OCCURRING

OVULATORY

POST MENSTRUAL

PRE MENSTRUAL

FEMALE DESIRE_____

MALE DESIRE (no intercourse)__ __ __ __ __ __

FIGURE 13

Not everyone agrees that female desire is influenced by the menstrual cycle. Whatever the reason, though, feedback from couples indicates that many of them experience times when the wife can't keep up with her husband sexually. When there is a basic gap between them, it can be widened by many influences. The wife's libido can be further depressed by physical things that happen to her, but not to her husband — pregnancy, the post-partum adjustment period, menopause, being on "The Pill." At the same time, there are many other things that tend to inhibit sexual function — alcohol, fatigue, fear of pregnancy, preoccupation, distractions, depression, hostility (the list could go on and on). Someone with a strong sexual drive can function in spite of such influences — while a weaker drive can be wiped out. So where the husband has a strong sexual drive, and the wife a weaker one, anything which interferes with sexual function will squash her weak drive and leave his unaffected. The end result is that there can be times in a marriage when a wife feels unresponsive much, or even most, of the time. Her husband may desire intercourse two, four, five times a week, while she might be interested perhaps once a month — or even less. If she has three children under three years of age and is pregnant she is probably quite willing to forget the whole thing for the duration.

Because so many couples run into this situation at some stage in their marriages, we're going to spend some time looking at it. But before doing that we have just a word to those of you who are in the opposite situation where it's the husband who can't keep up with his wife when it comes to sexual interest and energy. We invite you to apply what we say to your situation. You will probably find both differences and similarities, both of which can be food for thought and dialogue. By the way, your situation could change. Women who have been very interested in sex at one stage in their lives can become very disinterested later on, and vice versa.

Faced with a situation in which the wife can't begin to keep up with her husband, there are really only two possibilities, or a combination of the two. One is to limit intercourse to those times when the woman feels desire. In this case the husband may wonder why he didn't join the Trappists; at least it would have been quieter! The other alternative is for intercourse to take place sometimes when the woman feels no desire. This is non-erotic intercourse.

Let's take a look at these two possibilities. How about settling it with **male continence alone?** (No intercourse unless the wife feels desire, no matter how seldom this is.) Male readers have probably figured out that there are some objections to this policy. First of all, it involves real hardship for the man. Women are sometimes dumb about this. Because it's not bothering them, they assume that it should not be bothering their husbands. But that is not the way things work. Another objection we have is that we think it's **unfair.** It assumes that this relationship should be tailored to meet the needs of only one partner. If the other doesn't fit into that arrangement, that is just his tough luck.

But what we want to emphasize is that we believe that this practice is **dangerous to the husband-wife relationship.**

How dangerous depends on whose idea it is. If it is the wife's idea, if she is imposing continence on her husband, it is very dangerous indeed, a real recipe for disaster. This takes us back to something we emphasized in Chapter 4. A man's primary instinctive love-need is to be appreciated and accepted sexually. If he doesn't feel loved here, he won't feel loved at all. There is nothing else that can so quickly poison a man's attitude toward his wife as feeling rejected, abused and humiliated in this relationship. The tragic thing is that this can happen without his wife having a clue as to what's going on. It's not important to her, and she doesn't realize what it's doing to him. She feels his hostility, but doesn't guess its source.

If it's the husband's idea — if for some reason he accepts this semi-celibate lifestyle freely, the situation is less dangerous but, we think, not without danger. A warm and lively sexual relationship makes it much easier for a husband to love his wife. When it comes to loving, most of us can use all the help we can get. It makes loving easier because it taps that powerful instinctive love-sex source. If a man is cut off from this source, there is much more danger that he will lose himself in outside activities while the marriage becomes an empty shell, without much life or warmth. Incidentally, this also applies to situations where, for some reason, it is the husband who neglects this relationship.

We are not suggesting that continence has no place. We have stressed that an essential element in the art of seduction is wisdom in choosing the right time and the right place. By the time a husband has waited for or arranged for the right time and place, he usually has exercised a lot of restraint. But we do suggest that in marriages where there is a big gap in erotic need and capacity between husband and wife it is not very wise to try to resolve the problem with male continence alone.

What about the **alternative — intercourse taking place without desire on the part of the wife?** Can this be a healthy solution? It depends, because the psychological quality of intercourse without desire can vary enormously. Let's look at four different situations.

PSYCHOLOGICAL RAPE

Circumstances	Attitude	Response	Feeling	Long-Range Effect on Erotic Potential
External Compulsion — "Marriage Duty" — Psychological Pressure — Marital Blackmail	Psychological rape	Forced submission	Anger Contempt for husband	Destructive Sex = Violation Sex role bitterness

FIGURE 14

The first of these situations we call "psychological rape." "Rape" because intercourse is being forced on the wife. "Psychological" because the pressure being used is not a physical force, but some kind of psychological pressure. It was very common in the past with the concept of marriage duty. It was a mortal sin if women said "No." More often nowadays, it takes the form of marital blackmail. He won't be nice to her mother, or he won't take the kids to the circus. Or he will just be so generally rotten to live with that she reluctantly yields to his pressure in order to buy a few days of civility around the house. So her response is one of forced submission. Her feelings are ones of anger and contempt for her husband. The experience goes into her memory bank as a bad sexual memory. Sex as violation. She is bitter about the role that forces her into this situation. She is likely to conclude that "it's a man's world."

This situation is obviously a total disaster, destructive both of love and of the wife's capacity for enjoying sex. A love relationship between two people is unlikely to survive when one is being raped, the other treated as a rapist. And even a few experiences like this, especially if they come early in a woman's sexual experience, can leave such vivid and bitter memories in her memory bank that it will be a long haul up hill for her to develop any positive feelings about sex.

The commonest causes of this situation in the past were ignorance and mis-education. Even now, these play a part. Sometimes it develops due to serious personality problems. But most often nowadays this "rape" situation is the result of selfishness on the part of one, or the other, or both — usually both, because selfishness is contagious. The man says, "I want what I want when I want it." And the woman says, "I don't want what I don't want when I don't want it." Neither is being other-centered enough to care about, or even notice, the other's needs and feelings.

THE MARTYR

Circumstances	Attitude	Response	Feeling	Long-Range Effect on Erotic Potential
Sense of obligation (justice) Underdeveloped love (lacks knowledge, understanding, faith in husband)	Duty The Martyr The "Good Wife" who "never refuses" her husband	Resigned co-operation	Irritation (nuisance) Alienation from husband	Destructive Sex = Chore (irksome resented) Sex role resentment

FIGURE 15

In Figure 15, we look at a second situation involving non-erotic intercourse. Here the wife experiences **sexual intimacy as a duty,** and her attitude toward this duty is that of **a martyr.** The martyr is still a victim, suffering at the hands of another. But now she is a heroic victim; she suffers for a good cause. She may claim that she's putting up with this cross because she loves her husband, even though he's a "dog." (It usually takes about 10 seconds to get across the message that he is quite unworthy of her.) Some women say that they are putting up with this husband's sexual demands because of the children. They intend to hang in there until the children are educated and away from home. Sometimes they even have the gall to blame God for it and call it "their marriage duty." The ones that really confuse us are the ones who seem to suffer willingly in this situation. They say, "He gets it once a month" — sort of every first Friday. You get the impression that sex is some sort of substitute for the Stations of the Cross. She says, "He gets it once a month, but there is really nothing in it for me." And she smiles and feels very virtuous. What she doesn't realize is that with an attitude like this, there is very little in it for her husband either, because his needs are not being met.

So what doesn't she know about his needs? She doesn't know, for instance, that the reason sex is so important to him is that it has deep, profound psychological meaning, because sexual acceptance is **his basic love-need.** So when she hands out sex grudgingly — or even willingly, but sort of impersonally like when you get your oil changed or air in your spare tire — her husband is left empty, unfulfilled, frustrated and lonely. And, most dangerous of all, he is left insulted. He is insulted because he is not being accepted sexually; he is barely being tolerated. And, this again threatens his love source and he is not at all sure that she really loves him. He is looking for much more than tolerance. **He is looking for affection, physical warmth, closeness and tenderness. He is looking for interest, that is, a real tangible concern for himself as a person. He is looking for acceptance and appreciation of himself, as a man.** He is certainly looking for some tangible sign of caring on her part. So when his sexual needs routinely take on less importance than her *Time* magazine, the newspaper or her new hairdo, when his needs are being taken care of quickly as the last act of the day, he hears her say very distinctly, "Sure I love you. Sure I care — but not that much."

She must remember that virility is not a disease. It is not like acne or the seven-year itch. He won't outgrow it or get over it. Virility is part of him as a man and, if she doesn't love it, she doesn't love him. He needs to be needed and wanted, not just to carry out the garbage and do up her zipper, or chase away the mice that keep attacking her. He needs to be needed sexually and wanted sexually. A woman's initiative is very important here. He needs to know and be told these things, just as women do, that right here and right now, he is the most important person in the world — not treated as one of the kids that she can't quite handle or one of the pets that is resistant to housebreaking.

This martyr situation is obviously a damaging one for several reasons. The first is that she already has this negative attitude toward sex and each episode of sexual intercourse makes it worse. It's one more bad memory for her memory bank. Secondly, it splits the husband/wife relationship right down the middle, because it destroys the instinctive love source for both of them. The wife feels abused and, therefore, unloved. He feels rejected and, therefore, unloved. So, in this situation, each sexual episode is seen as evidence that the partner doesn't love. This is the exact opposite of what should be taking place. What should be a special way of loving has now become a special curse. Growth is not possible. A cold war is almost inevitable.

The causes for it are much the same as for psychological rape. There is still a certain amount of ignorance. Commonly we meet a rigidity in both the husband and the wife. They say, "That is the way I am." Somehow, that is supposed to end the discussion as if there is nothing more they can or will consider doing to change the situation.

Part of it always comes back to selfishness because there is no attempt to put oneself inside the other's skin, to feel the other's feelings, to try and understand the other's needs and wants or even to question one's own judgment. Basic to it all is that they are living with imperfect love. They both lack many of the characteristics of love. They don't have the trust, respect, knowledge or faith in each other. They do not have giving and acceptance of each other. So, very quickly begins the negative cycle that we talked about earlier. And if this negative cycle can't be broken, the marriage is inevitably going to drift downhill all the way.

In Figure 16, we see the beginning of a third situation. This lady starts out to be an ideal sexual partner, both for her husband's sake and for the sake of her marriage. This is quite a different attitude from the previous two women. It seems that this lady knows a few things that the others didn't. For one thing she understands that her husband's sexual needs are human, not animal; so she has to come up with a warm, affectionate and enthusiastic response before

73

she can consider herself a good wife. And she is aware of the importance of this relationship in her marriage. She knows how much a good sexual relationship can do for a marriage, and she is not about to waste this tool. Dr. Marian Hilliard, an obstetrician and gynecologist, has this advice to offer her female patients (we stress the fact that she was talking to women, because this would not be good advice to give to men). "The way to save a strained marriage, I advise my patients, is to start with the act of love." (She is referring here to sexual intercourse.) "Here are the essentials of marriage in concentrated form. In one act are consideration, warmth, gaiety, charm, hunger and ecstasy. In this small kingdom, a woman can heal the wounds caused by indifference and contempt. She is a fool, if she ignores this tool provided her by nature." Dr. Hilliard adds: **"If women spent half the time cultivating the sexual relationship that they sometimes spend avoiding it, their marriages would blossom."** And someone has offered this beautitude for an ever-warm marriage: "Blessed is the wife who can celebrate (and we like that word 'celebrate') her husband's virility with a true generosity that often seeks not so much to be loved as to love."

So this woman starts out to be an ideal sexual partner — even if it kills her. And, as we see in Figure 17 it just about does. She gets involved in what we call a **"labor of love."** She will force an erotic response, or perish in the attempt. Of course, it can't be done, because erotic feelings cannot be forced. As soon as you start working at sex, erotic feeling

LABOR OF LOVE

Circumstances	Attitude
Determination to be an "ideal" sexual partner — for husband's sake — for sake of marriage	"Labor of love"

FIGURE 16

74

goes out the window. Working at sex doesn't work. So her efforts to force a response instead of narrowing the gap in sexual interest between her and her husband make it wider instead. Sex becomes a task, and then, a hopeless task. Instead of being fun for her it is one big headache — a source of feelings of anxiety, inadequacy, guilt and failure. The whole thing has become a nightmare in which erotic feelings will never arise. She will be tempted to slip back into the martyr or psychological-rape situation.

The mistake this woman has made is in assuming that the only way she can meet her husband's needs is by matching him orgasm for orgasm. This is a peculiarly modern problem for two reasons. First of all, there is the modern obsesssion with technical performance: with things like attaining orgasm, producing erections, achieving multiple orgasms, postponing the husband's orgasm, simultaneous orgasm. Couples are so anxious about their performance and achieving all these things that the really important things get lost — things like freedom, affection, humor, playfulness, fun and love.

The first and most fundamental element in sexual therapy is to free couples from this pressure to perform — to set them free simply to enjoy sexual intimacy without worrying about all these technical factors.

The other reason we are running into this problem more often today is the modern tendency to impose masculine

LABOR OF LOVE

Circumstances	Attitude	Response	Feeling	Long-Range Effect on Erotic Potential
Determination to be an "ideal" sexual partner — for husband's sake — for sake of marriage	"Labor of love"	Struggle to force an erotic response Failing that — pretense	Effort, frustration Dishonesty	Destructive Sex = Problem Sex = Work Sense of inadequacy, failure as woman

FIGURE 17

standards of sexual fulfillment on women. It is assumed that, because masculine sexual fulfillment always takes the same form, the same should be true of women. We have gone to the opposite extreme from the Victorians who assumed that women were entirely different, sexually, from men. We tend to expect them to be exactly the same. The truth is probably somewhere in between.

Sometimes it is the wife who gets herself into this box. But sometimes it is the husband who, with the best of intentions, pushes her into it. This is a quotation from a young wife who came to a marriage counselor for help because her husband kept insisting that there was only one manner of sex satisfaction — and of course that was his. This gal said, "I wish he would quit pressing me to get as excited as he does. I could enjoy it so much more if he would let me enjoy the closeness while he enjoys the excitement. Is it so wrong for me sometimes to think of sex purely as my ministry to his needs? Must I always feel like he feels?" We think this lady hits the nail right on the head. We do not know of any law that says that a woman's pleasure and fulfillment in sexual intercourse has to be measured in orgasms. The fact is that a loving and mature woman can enjoy sexual intercourse in many different ways. For one thing, she should be able to express in this relationship the very powerful maternal part of her sexuality. The young wife we quoted mentioned one aspect of this, her joy in ministering to her husband's needs.

But perhaps even deeper is the maternal joy in giving life. There is a very close bond between the marriage bed and the delivery table in more ways than one. On both a woman can give life. In the marriage bed she can restore her husband, renew his confidence in himself, give him new zest and joy in life and at the same time bring new life and warmth into the marriage and into the home.

This capacity for enjoying sexual intercourse in many different ways is an essential part of feminine sexuality. So much so, that a woman can become very frustrated sexually if she is only allowed to develop and express herself in an erotic way. Sexual fulfillment in a woman requires that she be **free** — free to be herself, free to express her love, her tenderness, her creativity, her total sexuality in whatever way that, at the moment, comes naturally to her (see Figure 18). This may sometimes mean a full erotic response with orgasm; sometimes a partial erotic response without orgasm; and sometimes a response in which there is little or no erotic feeling but which is still deeply sexual, deeply sensual and deeply fulfilling for her.

LOVE FREELY EXPRESSED

Circumstances	Attitude	Response	Feeling	Long-Range Effect on Erotic Potential
Sense of freedom to "be herself" in making love Impossible without husband's acceptance	Love freely expressed	Spontaneous response with no preconceived goal	Joyful, intimacy. Creative fulfillment May or may not take an erotic "turn"	Constructive Sex = Fun Sex = Play Pleased with herself as woman

FIGURE 18

Where a woman has this freedom to be herself in making love, and where there is an other-centered love to express, a difference in sexual appetite isn't an insoluble problem. Sexual intercourse can be enjoyed and lived on many different levels. Some women even report that they are most deeply moved when the erotic element is absent.

Now, just briefly, let's consider those marriages where the shoe is on the other foot, where it is the husband who can't keep up with his wife when it comes to sexual energy. Exactly the same principles apply. With a little imagination you can translate and imagine the man in each of these situations too. Again, the important thing is that he be able to function at that last level — "love, freely expressed," a level of freedom and relaxed play, without any worries about performance.

One difference, of course, is that, when a man can't quite get an erection, coitus is impossible. We again want to remind you that there is nothing abnormal about occasional impotence. It is to be expected in a situation where the wife has a stronger drive than her husband. There will be times when she is interested in coitus and he would love to oblige, because he loves her. But it is just not possible; he just doesn't have as much go-power as she has. As long as the couple doesn't get into a flap about it, it is not a big deal. Physical affection is always possible, as well as all kinds of sexual play other than coitus. And a wife doesn't need coitus to reach orgasm. In fact, direct stimulation of the clitoris is actually more effective. So the key to living with this situation — just as much as the reverse one — is for the husband to allow himself to function at that last level, the level of love, freely expressed.

CHAPTER 10

WE BELIEVE

Our concern in this book has been with the "nitty-gritty" of marital sexuality — with the very down-to-earth ways in which we are challenged to put the principles of love into practice in our sexual interaction. We don't want to leave the subject without witnessing to our conviction that we miss the whole point of human love and sexuality unless we see them in the context of a larger mystery — the mystery of God and His love.

We believe that human love is Divine love translated into human experience. In God's plan, the first human love, the source of all others, is the love of husband and wife. It is of the essence of this relationship that it is a **sexual** relationship — "male and female, He created them."

Sexuality is at the core of God's plan for marriage. We believe that we understand this plan only to the degree that we understand our own sexuality, our partner's sexuality and the ways in which they interact in the day-to-day events of married life.

It is not by accident that God made us male and female. He made us different and yet very much alike, physically and emotionally, so that we could delight in each other's differences and rejoice in what we share — that we could marvel at what we lack and glory in what we can build together — that with all this variety of fuel, the fires of our love would never falter. In and through all this, He prepares us for our initiation into His own life, which is also a mystery of diversity in unity.

If we don't understand our sexuality, or if we can't accept it, we are guaranteed heartache in our intimate life, confusion and mediocrity in family and community life. Worst of all, we are missing the path by which God invites us to find our way home to Him.

The special sign and celebration of the unique love of husband and wife is the union of two in one flesh. We are distressed when we hear Christians label sexual intercourse "physical," or even "genital," or "pelvic" — as if it were something that takes place between two sets of detached reproductive organs. Nothing is more psychosomatic than the union of two in one flesh; that's why we have to take issues of sexual morality so seriously. Sexual intercourse is always a kind of natural sacrament between the two persons involved; it both expresses and creates the quality of their relationship. It can be a sacrament of all kinds of things — hedonism, hatred, exploitation, love; but it can never be merely "physical." It is always a sign that "effects what it signifies." How vital, then, that we seek to perfect it as a sign of love. How much more important that we do so if we are Christians, for whom Christ has raised this natural sacrament to the supernatural plane.

We know that sexual intimacy has given us many beautiful, joyous, cherished experiences. We're sure God has designed it to do so, as a sign of how much He loves us — that this is a special gift from our Father that He wants us all to understand and to enjoy to the full. We believe this special sign of His love is really part of the Good News that Christians are asked to share and to spread — to pass on to our children and others — to show that God is alive, and that He loves us, and that He cares for each of us in a very personal and specific way.

We believe our Father is just as fascinated by our sex lives as He is by our prayer lives. We think He's sad when our sex lives are inadequate, disappointed when we don't make them full and free and joy-filled. And we're sure He's delighted when we have a ball, using all His gifts to delight each other and to glorify Him by becoming "men and women fully alive." After all, He is the Father who sent His Son to the cross so that we might have life in abundance. This abundant life is what we are striving for as we try to perfect our sexuality and to make our love for each other more Christlike, more attuned to the Father's dream for us.

We can't imagine a healthy sex life — or a holy one — without a lot of laughs. Sexual intercourse isn't a big project at which we must succeed, nor is it an occasion for pseudo-religious solemnity. We believe it should be a joyful meeting of two relaxed people in love, who freely and eagerly give and take and share some of life's most sublime moments. It's a time for fun, for relaxation, for laughter. It can also be a time for moments of our most intense prayer; prayer of thanksgiving for such great joy and pleasure, prayer of adoration as momentarily we glimpse a wispy shadow of the Reality that is to be ours forever.

We believe that there is more at stake in our sexual interaction than our own happiness and wholeness. The quality of our relationship as husband and wife determines the quality of presence we will bring to the world outside our home. We won't bring peace to the world if there's a war on at home! Even more important, it determines the quality of life we will generate in our children, and the kind of community our family will be.

For Christians, this has implications that transcend psychological values. Christian marriage has been consecrated as a fountainhead of God's own life and love in the world; the family is "the domestic Church." God invites the Christian husband to love his wife the way Christ loves the Church, spending himself for her. He invites the Christian wife to love her husband the way the Church loves Christ — to have in him the faith, the hope, and the joy that the Church has in Christ. And He promises us: "If you two struggle to love each other in this way, I will share My life with you. I will take your human love, and transform it into My love. I will take your human life together, and transform it into My life." And so this earthly trinity that we call marriage — husband, wife and God — becomes, not just a reflection of the Trinity (which it has been from the beginning), but a sharing in the life of the Trinity; it becomes a new incarnation, a new making present in the flesh, of God's own life and love.

This is the quality of life that Christian spouses are empowered to generate in each other, in our families, in our church, and in the world. In the words of Father Gabriel Calvo, the originator of Marriage Encounter, "There is within each couple a divine energy of love, and if it can be brought alive, it can loose a true revolution of love over the whole earth."

81

Appendix

APPENDIX

Summaries & Dialogue Questions — for use
in workshops and seminars

A. Important Areas of Difference (Chapters 3, 4, & 5)

1. **Infidelity (Chronic Selfishness) wears different disguises.**
   (Chapter 3)
2. **Different relationship between Sex & Love.** (Chapter 4)

	MALE	FEMALE
Primary Instinctive Love Source	Love/Sex	Love/Protection Love/Security Love/Cooperation
Primary Instinctive Love Need	Sexual Acceptance	Protection Security Valued

which can lead to:

Either	Or

Wife **rejects** husband sexually   Wife's sex-drive becomes **weaker**   Wife's sex-drive becomes **stronger**   Wife **accepts** husband sexually

N E G A T I V E CYCLE   **P O S I T I V E** CYCLE

Husband feels **hostile, neglects** wife   Husband feels **warmth,** is **considerate, friendly** toward wife

3. **Different patterns of response in relation to Sexual Intercourse:** (Chapter 5)
   (a) In the young couple.   (b) In the later years.

Questions for Dialogue

1. Is there anything in my partner's sexuality that I find difficult to accept? What feelings on my part cause this difficulty?

2. Do I have the impression that there is anything in my own sexuality that is not accepted by my partner?
   How does this make me feel?

B. Love (Chapter 7)

Some Characteristics of Love

1. Love is a Faculty, an Art.

2. Love is Other-centered — shown by
   — **Respect**
   — **Unconditional Acceptance**
   — **Knowledge — Understanding**
   — **Communication**
   — **Giving — Responsibility — Care**

3. Love Seeks Union — but on the condition that each person remains whole & fully himself or herself (Union with Integrity)

4. Love is Honest, Real.

5. Love includes Faith, Hope.

Some "Facts of Love"

I must love myself before I can love others.

Healthy love of others is rooted in healthy self-love.

"Love your neighbor as yourself."

Love can't be demanded; it is a free response. Love dies in a climate of chronic indifference and neglect.

People tend to become what we tell them they are.

"We grow only for people who believe in us, who trust us, who love us."

We learn to love by being loved.

Love doesn't keep score.

Love is contagious (so are indifference and selfishness). Because of this, growth in love in marriage is a mutual affair — a team effort — and husbands and wives usually end up deserving each other.

Love is a decision.

Questions for Dialogue

1. In what characteristic of love would I especially like to grow? How could my partner help me to grow in this characteristic?

2. In what characteristic of love would I especially like to see my partner grow? How could I help him/her to grow in this characteristic?

C. The Art of Seduction (Chapter 8)

I. Psychological Seduction: Important Aspects

— **Climate of Love**
— **Emotional Bridge**
— **Wisdom — in selecting time & place**
— **Memory Bank full of good sexual memories**
— **Personal experience — affection, romance**

Questions for Dialogue

1. What can I do to improve our love-making in the area of psychological seduction?
2. What can my partner do?

II. Physical Seduction: Important Aspects

— **Foreplay — not forework**
— **Unhuried progress**
— **Artful stimulation of erogenous zones**
     artful = lightness of touch & variety
— **Partner's desire should lead other partner's caresses**
— **Be guided by partner's responses**
— **Partner's responsibility — to communicate — to participate**

Questions for Dialogue

1. What can I do to improve our love-making in the area of physical seduction?
2. What can my partner do?

****

TERMS

****

Foreplay — The gentle caressing (touching, "tickling") of erogenous zones.

Erogenous Zones — Parts of the body that, when touched, give sexual pleasure and awaken sexual desire. However, they do this only if they are touched in the right way and at the right time (when the person is in the right mood). All the body surfaces are mildly erogenous. However, some parts are especially erogenous.

Strongly Erogenous Zones — Lips
Breasts (especially the nipples)
Inner thighs
Lower Abdomen
Buttocks

Intensely Erogenous Zones — The genital (sexual) organs of both sexes.

Male — Penis, scrotum (containing testicles)
Female — The whole area between the labia ("lips") of the vulva
Especially — The clitoris
The introitus ("entrance") of the vagina
The vesituble ("hall")
area between the clitoris and introitus.

87

D. When Sexual Appetites Differ (Chapter 9)

NON-EROTIC SEXUAL INTERCOURSE IN WOMEN

Circumstances	Attitude	Response	Feeling	Long-Range Effect on Erotic Potential
External Compulsion – "Marriage Duty" – Psychological Pressure – Marital Blackmail	Psychological rape	Forced submission	Anger Contempt for husband	Destructive Sex = Violation Sex role bitterness
Sense of obligation (justice) – Underdeveloped love (lacks knowledge, understanding, faith in husband)	Duty The martyr The "good wife" who "never refuses" her husband.	Resigned Cooperation	Irritation (Nuisance) Alienation from husband	Destructive Sex = Chore (irksome, resented)

			Destructive	Destructive
Determine to be an "ideal" sexual partner — for husband's sake — for sake of marriage	"Labor of Love"	Struggle to force an erotic response Failing that — pretense	Effort, frustration Dishonesty	Sex = Problem Sex = Work Sense of inadequacy, failure as woman
Sense of freedom to "be herself" in making love. Impossible without husband's acceptance	Love freely expressed	Spontaneous response, with no pre-conceived goal.	Joyful intimacy, creative fulfillment May or may not take an erotic "turn"	CONSTRUCTIVE Sex = Fun Sex = Play Pleased with herself as woman.

Questions for Dialogue

1. The above outline describes four situations: "Psychological Rape," "Duty," "Labor of Love," "Love Freely Expressed." Do we, as a couple, come close to fitting one of these descriptions? If so, which one? Adapt the question, if, in your case, it is the wife who has the heartier sexual appetite.

2. What could be done to make our sexuality a more effective channel of love? What could I do? What could my partner do? What could we do as a couple?

89